# Now Entering Weirdsville!

## The Strangest Stories You've Ever Heard

D1649062

Written by Andrea Urton

Illustrated by Will Suckow

Lowell House

Juvenile

Los Angeles

**Contemporary Books**

Chicago

*To Amy, Lisa, and Lisa—*
*all members of the Weirdsville town council*
—A. U.

*To my loving parents,*
*with whom weirdness is no stranger*
—W. S.

Cover illustration by John Dickenson
Interior design by Brenda Leach

Manufactured in the United States of America

ISBN: 1-56565-024-7
Registered with the Library of Congress

10 9 8 7 6 5 4 3 2

# CONTENTS

# Do you DARE go to WEIRDSVILLE?

A headless corpse baking in the Arizona desert . . . a simple housewife on her hands and knees scrubbing to remove phantom faces from the floor . . . a tiny creature carrying a combustion chamber within its own body . . . these and many more are the citizens of Weirdsville. Around every corner and lurking in every shadowy doorway is another mystery, another oddity, or another example of the unpredictability of fate.

But these are not stories penned simply to amuse a visitor. The tales of Weirdsville are true. Each and every one is verified by reliable witnesses, researchers, historians, police detectives, or even heads of state. What caused a flight of Navy bombers to disappear from a cloudless sky? Who was the lone sailor riding the bow of a German submarine before it exploded into bits? What waits at the bottom of the money pit of Oak Island? If you wish to discover the answers, you must gather your courage and join the tour . . .

# Welcome to Weirdsville!

# The Phantoms of Bélmez

You might expect to find a ghost gliding through the halls of an ancient British manor. And believers wouldn't be surprised to encounter a restless spirit on a shadowy country road in New England. But in 1971, a housewife in Bélmez, Spain, was astonished to find a phantom face on her kitchen floor! Maria Pereira didn't know the identity of the woman whose image had suddenly appeared in broad daylight. At first Maria did her best to scrub the image from the tiles, but it resisted her efforts. In fact, the more she scrubbed, the sadder the expression on the face became, and it seemed to open its eyes wider with each stroke.

Terrified, she had the entire floor taken up and a new covering of concrete poured in its place. Less than three weeks later, the face returned, and others followed. Some would appear for only a short period. Others would remain, but their tormented expressions would change over time. The uncanny apparitions attracted a great deal of attention. Mrs. Pereira allowed tourists to visit her kitchen, and soon dozens of people were witness to the bizarre "haunting."

Eventually, the authorities stepped in to investigate. The

kitchen was sealed off, and scientists set to work to discover the origin of the spectacle. To be certain that no one was secretly drawing the faces, they had a large plastic plate fitted to the floor. Even so, the images continued to emerge. A section of floor was removed, and the images were chemically tested for any artificial pigments. The results were negative. In 1974, a Spanish professor actually witnessed the formation of one of the configurations and was able to photograph it in detail.

Finally, there was nothing left to do but dig up the floor and discover whatever might lurk beneath it. When workmen removed the stone and began to excavate the soil, they discovered ancient bones perhaps as much as 900 years old ...human bones. Although it has never been proven, some townsfolk claimed that the kitchen had been built over the site of a cemetery. The bodies below were thought to be either those of eleventh-century martyrs killed by Moorish invaders, or innocent victims who had been accused of witchcraft and executed.

After the discovery of the bones, and even with an entirely new floor in place, the faces continued to appear. One expert brought in sensitive microphones designed to detect sounds beyond the range of human hearing. When the tapes were played back, the researchers heard

Not just President Lincoln but also his funeral train are said to have reappeared for a time. Beginning in 1866, the year after Lincoln's assassination, the train was witnessed every April 27 (the date Lincoln's body was carried on the train) for several years. It materialized on an area of track near Albany, New York. The original train passed that way when carrying the fallen president's body from Washington to Illinois.

moans and tortured, mournful voices wailing in unfamiliar languages.

Scientists were completely baffled. Eventually, the phenomenon ended as suddenly as it had begun. Although many people have theories about the cause, none has ever been proven. The purpose of the mysterious phantom faces of Bélmez remains a secret.

# The Power of Love

In 1912, Juliette Gordon Low formed the first Girl Scout troop in the United States. Today, you can tour her childhood home in Savannah, Georgia. Known as the Juliette Gordon Low Girl Scout National Center, or simply "The Birthplace," it was that city's first national monument.

Ever since the home was opened to the public, several people have reported that once the daily visitors are gone, Nellie Kinzie Gordon, Juliette's mother, reclaims her stately home. On one occasion, a tour guide encountered Mrs. Gordon in the upstairs hall. The guide claimed the "ghost" seemed as startled as she was to run into someone. A maintenance man states that he has seen Mrs. Gordon at the dining-room table, wearing a long blue robe adorned with a pattern of delicate flowers. And, although the antique piano is no longer in working order, this same witness also reports having heard music from the parlor. Mrs. Gordon was said to be fond of playing the piano.

Actually, the first spirit reported to have been seen in the home was not that of Nellie but of her husband, William. He supposedly appeared on the day of Nellie's death: February 22, 1917.

The Gordons were a proud family, with

*In* 1924, two sailors on the SS *Watertown* were killed in an accident and buried at sea. Throughout the balance of the journey, however, they were spotted by many crew members, who said the two men were swimming after the ship. The captain was actually able to photograph the men, and their faces are visible in the print.

*Not all ghosts* are human. On the Isle of Man in the Irish Sea, there is said to be a *phantom weasel.* According to those who claim to have seen it, it can imitate the calls of a number of other animals, including humans.

8

a fine history that stretched back to the Revolutionary War. Their Savannah home was built in 1820, and the first of five generations of Gordons to live in the house was William Washington Gordon. His son, William II, was born there. In 1858, young William took Nellie Kinzie to be his wife. They were very much in love and remained devoted to each other throughout their lives together.

But life wasn't always easy. During the Civil War, Nellie's family fought on the side of the Union forces. William was a Confederate officer in the Georgia Hussars. The couple was separated toward the end of the war when Nellie was forced to take the children north for their safety. In 1865 the family was reunited.

After the war, William went on to distinguish himself as a soldier in the service of his country, eventually becoming a brigadier general. Nellie, who worked with ailing soldiers, was known as a woman with a mind of her own who was not afraid to stand up for what she believed in. Both were admired and respected, and no one ever questioned their great love for each other.

When William died in 1912, the city of Savannah mourned the loss. Nellie, however, was convinced that this was merely yet another separation that she would have to endure. She was certain that William would come back so they could be together again. She requested that

▲

*The spirit world doesn't neglect the highways. There are many stories of hitchhiking ghosts. The phantoms include a troubled young blond girl on the Skyway Bridge in Central Florida, and an 11-year-old boy who flags down a ride near his former school near Tulsa, Oklahoma. Drivers report talking to the ghosts, but the apparitions generally disappear.*

▼

when she died, no one wear black at her funeral. It would instead be a happy time, since she would be reunited with her beloved husband.

According to several eyewitnesses, she was right. Nellie's five surviving children had been with her when she died. They all commented that she seemed extremely happy and content. Her niece, Daisy Gordon Lawrence, later wrote that her radiant face was that of "a bride going to meet her bridegroom."

On the day of her death, the first to see the "bridegroom" was his daughter-in-law, Margaret. She claimed to have observed the general walking down the main staircase, splendidly dressed in his finest uniform. The family butler agreed. He watched from the lower level as General Gordon strolled calmly down the stairs and walked out the front door.

Can love survive beyond mortal boundaries? Perhaps "The Birthplace" is a monument not only to Juliette Gordon Low, but also to the devotion of her parents.

# The Faithful
# L·I·E·U·T·E·N·A·N·T

During World War I, the submarine was a fearful weapon. A crew could slip within range of an enemy ship and destroy it without ever surfacing. German forces put hundreds of Unterseebooten (oon-ter-see-BOOT-en)—or U-boats—into service. Most were fairly large, but about two dozen smaller craft were launched in 1916. Each carried a crew of 31. Among this smaller fleet was the U-65.

The reputation of the U-65 as being an ill-fated vessel began even before she was completed. During construction, two workmen were crushed when a huge metal girder slipped from its place. Three others choked to death on toxic fumes when a door to the engine room jammed shut during sea trials.

Just before the U-65 made her first test dive, a young sailor was drowned. A witness claimed that the man seemed to simply walk into the water. He did not call for help and made no attempt to swim. The captain chose to go through with the test. He intended to dive to the bottom and surface within a few minutes. The submarine sank to the bottom, and that is where she stayed for 12 terrifying hours. The crew survived the ordeal—but the U-65's legacy of death was far from over. Once back in port she was loaded with supplies, along with a full load of

In 1541, the Countess of Salisbury was slated to be another victim of execution at the Tower of London. As she was led toward her doom, however, she struggled free and ran away. The executioner caught her and parted her head from her neck with a huge ax. According to modern-day witnesses, the gruesome scene is sometimes replayed in every detail on the tower grounds.

torpedoes. As the last torpedo was being eased into place, it exploded. Five men lost their lives. Among them was the ship's second officer, a lieutenant.

The U-65 was badly damaged in the blast and needed extensive repairs. When she was finally ready and the crew had boarded, the ship's petty officer dutifully counted each man—but he counted more than he bargained for. Frightened, he reported to the captain that the dead second officer had reported for duty. A search turned up nothing, but the petty officer was not the only man to have seen the phantom. Over the next few months, official reports mentioned several sightings of him on board, standing at the prow of the vessel. Apparently, the lieutenant wished to continue serving aboard the U-65, even after death!

On one occasion, three crew members also saw the ghostly figure standing on the prow. Convinced that the sighting heralded disaster, the captain was relieved when the ship cruised safely into port. His relief was unjustified. He was killed in an air raid that very evening.

The new captain assigned to the U-65 had heard of the ship's reputation. He tried to ease the fears of his nervous crew by conducting a thorough investigation into all of the strange reports of ghostly appearances and untimely deaths. A priest was brought on board to drive away any spirits that might haunt the boat. But once the U-65 was out to sea, a

**THE UNITED STATES**

has its own "royal" ghosts. Abraham Lincoln has been seen in the White House by a personage no less impressive than Queen Wilhelmina of the Netherlands. She told others that she had answered a knock at her door, only to find Lincoln standing there. The queen promptly fainted. Others who claimed to have seen Lincoln's spirit include Theodore Roosevelt and Sir Winston Churchill.

young sailor reportedly leaped from the deck and drowned. Another was washed overboard.

The lieutenant continued to appear. The most bizarre report, however, came not from the log of the U-65 but from the captain of a U.S. submarine that had attempted to sink the U-65 as it was cruising just at the surface. As the captain of the American sub was preparing to fire, the U-65 suddenly exploded. The actual cause of the explosion remains a mystery, locked in the depths of the sea. The story of the U-65 had come to an end, but with one incredible footnote: The American captain claimed that when he had the German submarine in his periscope sights, he saw a lone figure standing calmly at the prow.

As the second wife of Henry VIII, **Anne Boleyn** was Queen of England. That didn't save her from being beheaded at the Tower of London. Her ghost, however, walks her childhood home at Blickling Hall just outside of London. She reportedly strolls in the garden and is sometimes seen carrying her severed head. Another of Henry's wives, Queen Catherine Howard, haunts Hampton Court near London. She is seen walking with a procession of ladies-in-waiting.

One day in 1826 near Melbourne, Australia, many people saw *a ghost* standing on a bridge and pointing to the creek below. The ghost vanished immediately after being seen. So many people witnessed the apparition that the area to which it pointed was dug up. There rested the bones of a man named Fred Fisher, who had apparently been the victim of a murder. The criminal was apprehended and the bones properly reburied. Although the phantom has not been seen since, the creek is known as Fisher's Ghost Creek.

One of the world's most "haunted" sites may be the **Tower of London.** For several hundred years, between 1100 and approximately 1941, many famous people were confined there. Until 1747, a great number of nobles, including several queens, were beheaded on the grounds. Among the prisoners was the dashing Sir Walter Raleigh, known for his chivalry toward, ladies. Reputedly, his phantom still walks the halls of the tower, and some tourists claim they have seen it. As you might expect, it is said to appear only to women.

Not all spirits seem to be harmful. At the Prince Albert Hospital in Sydney, Australia, there supposedly lives a ghost known as *the Good Sister.* She is the phantom of a nurse who died tragically in a fall at the hospital. Some employees say they still see her on her rounds. She is said to have actually aided a needy patient one evening by drawing attention to him. A nurse saw her bending over the patient and stepped forward to investigate. It turned out that the man needed immediate help. His condition might not have been noticed in time if it hadn't been for the Good Sister.

# TRAGIC LINKS

The names of Abraham Lincoln and John F. Kennedy are known throughout the world. As presidents of the United States, both of these men were powerful representatives of freedom and liberty. Sadly, both leaders fell at the hands of assassins.

The tragic deaths of these two men are marked by many strange coincidences. Lincoln began a term in Congress in 1847; Kennedy was elected to Congress exactly 100 years later. Lincoln became president of the United States in 1861; Kennedy began his term in office in 1961.

Andrew Johnson, a Southern politician, was Lincoln's vice president at the time of the assassination and became president after Lincoln's death. John F. Kennedy's vice president and successor in office was Lyndon Johnson, a Southern politician. Andrew Johnson was born in 1808; Lyndon Johnson was born in 1908.

Abraham Lincoln was shot on Friday, April 14, 1865, while seated next to his wife at a play at Ford's Theater in Washington, D.C. Only hours before, he had speculated on the possibility of such an attempt on his life. He had said to White House guard William Crook, "If it is to be done, it is impossible to prevent it." (Lincoln had reportedly mentioned to friends that he had dreamed of his own death. In the dream he had heard sobbing and seen many people in tears in the White House; when he asked a young soldier what had happened, he was told that the president had been assassinated.)

John Kennedy's secretary—Evelyn Lincoln—voiced misgivings about the president's trip to Dallas. Nevertheless, Kennedy made the trip and, on Friday, November 22, 1963, he reportedly commented, "If somebody wants to shoot me from a window with a rifle, nobody can stop it, so why worry about it?" That day, the fatal bullets allegedly burst from a high-powered rifle fired from a sixth-floor window. Kennedy was shot while riding in a motorcade. Oddly, the car in which he and his wife were passengers was a Lincoln.

The assassination of President Lincoln was carried out by a Southern-born man, John

ƻ

*American author Thomas Clayton Wolfe often told his editor that he proposed to write a story about the passengers in a railroad car. He planned to call it "K19," after the number of the fictional car. He never got around to it. Upon his death, Wolfe's body was shipped to North Carolina for burial. The number of the car in which the body was placed? K19.*

ƻ

Wilkes Booth. After firing a single shot, Booth ran from the theater and was said to have hidden in a storage barn. He was never brought to trial. Twelve days after the assassination, a man identified as Booth either shot himself or was shot by a soldier (the details are not clear) after the barn was set on fire.

Southern-born Lee Harvey Oswald, who many think shot President Kennedy, is said to have fired the shots from the window of a book-storage warehouse, then sought safety in a theater. Although apprehended, he was never brought to trial. Two days later, he, too, was shot.

Both Lincoln and Kennedy are said to be victims of a cycle known as the "fatal twenty," which began in 1840. In that year, William H. Harrison was elected president. He died in office one month later. From that time until 1980, the president elected to office every twentieth year died while in office (although not always during that term). Like the other two American presidents who died by assassination (James A. Garfield and William McKinley), Lincoln and Kennedy fit into the "fatal twenty" cycle. Is there some strange phenomenon at work here? It isn't likely. The circumstances actually fall within the realm of coincidence. In fact, the chain was broken in 1980, when Ronald Reagan became president. It should be noted, however, that during his first term President Reagan survived an attempt on his life.

# SETTLING THE SCORE

In 1880, the first ship fitted for refrigeration carried a cargo across the sea. The *Frigorifique* carried meat from France to many other European ports. It was the sad destiny of the *Frigorifique* to end her short career on the murky seafloor . . . but she would not be alone.

The fog was so dense on that fateful afternoon in 1884 that the ship could only creep forward. Those on deck strained to hear the sound of any other vessel cutting through the still water. The *Frigorifique* sounded her foghorn. A reply came moments later, but the warning was useless. The British ship *Rumney* was on a collision course with the *Frigorifique*. It slammed into the French vessel with tremendous force, slicing a gaping wound in her side. Seawater rushed into the boiler room, and the terrified crew scrambled for their lives. Luckily, the sailors aboard the *Rumney* managed to rescue the entire crew of the ill-fated ship.

Even as the Frenchmen were pulled to safety, the horror was far from over. Not far away, a ship slipped past, shrouded in mist. It was the *Frigorifique!* She vanished into the fog, then made another pass and this time lunged broadside into the *Rumney,* mortally wounding her. Battling for their lives, the French and British crews managed to squeeze into the *Rumney*'s lifeboats. Together they worked to row clear of the two ships.

As they drifted on the calm sea, moments later, the sailors' curiosity overcame their fear. One of the lifeboats edged closer to the *Frigorifique,* and several sailors boarded her. They soon found the reason for her return. After the collision, the wheel had been lashed to keep the *Frigorifique* on a circular course until she sank. After being abandoned, however, the ship had stopped taking on water. A single working boiler had kept her steaming in a wide circle, one that had made her collision with the *Rumney* inevitable.

Certain that the *Frigorifique* was now truly sinking, the sailors left her for the last time and returned to the safety of the lifeboat. The crews watched as the two ships disappeared into the gloom. The *Rumney* and the *Frigorifique* sank side by side, each having delivered the fatal blow to the other. Was it mere coincidence that the boiler on the *Frigorifique* continued to operate, and that the wheel had been lashed into a course that would aim the crippled ship at the heart of her executioner?

# Preview of MISFORTUNE

There is an old saying that truth is stranger than fiction. On the night of April 14, 1912, truth and fiction blended in a terrible and very real tragedy. In 1898, novelist Morgan Robertson had written the tale of a night of terror on the open sea. The book, *Futility*, was about the maiden voyage of a luxurious passenger ship called the *Titan*. To the shouted wishes of "Bon voyage," the fictional ship left the British port of Southampton on her way to New York. But it would never reach its destination. In the frigid North Atlantic, the *Titan* struck an immense iceberg. With a deep wound in her side, she sank swiftly. Because there were too few lifeboats, the *Titan* dragged hundreds of her passengers down with her. A sad tale, but then it was only fiction . . . or was it?

Fourteen years later, a ship similar in size and speed to the imaginary *Titan* embarked on her maiden voyage, also from Southampton to New York. Called the *Titanic*, she carried 2,224 persons. The ship was equipped with lifeboats for fewer than 1,200 people, but this was not considered to be a problem. The *Titanic* was said to be unsinkable.

Shortly before midnight on April 14, 1912, the *Titanic* was speeding through

In 1940, Warren Felty saved accident victim William Miller, who had been thrown from his car into a snowbank. In the winter of 1944, Felty was a prisoner of the Germans in Europe. He saved a fellow prisoner from freezing to death in a snowbank. Once again, it was William Miller.

*In the eleventh century,* a French priest became quite annoyed when a horde of buzzing flies kept interrupting his sermon. So, the man excommunicated the pesky insects. The following morning, hundreds of dead flies were removed from the church. The official explanation was that they had been killed by a severe frost.

the calm North Atlantic waters just south of Newfoundland at 22 knots, or roughly 25 miles per hour. Suddenly, an iceberg was sighted. The captain gave the order to turn, but it was too late. The tower of ice slashed a 300-foot-long gash in the ship's hull. Within two hours, 1,513 people had met watery deaths.

The bravery of the passengers and crew that terrible night is legendary. Survivors reported heroic efforts by the captain and his crew, who gave up their lives so others could survive. Even the ship's band played on and strains of music could be heard over the still, icy waters right up until the moment when the ship finally slipped beneath the surface.

There is still another chapter to the incredible union of fiction and reality in this tragic case. On the very day that the *Titanic* sank, a young man named William Reeves was born. On an April evening 23 years later, he was on watch on the deck of another ship that was plying the same North Atlantic waters that had claimed the *Titanic*. Reeves was familiar with the dreadful history. Sighting what he thought might be a perilous iceberg, he sounded the alarm. This time, a collision was narrowly avoided. The name of the fortunate ship on which Reeves was serving? The *Titanian*.

⇨ Over the course of his lifetime, a British officer named Summerford was **struck by lightning** three separate times. It didn't end there. Four years after his death, Summerford's tombstone was destroyed by lightning.

⇩

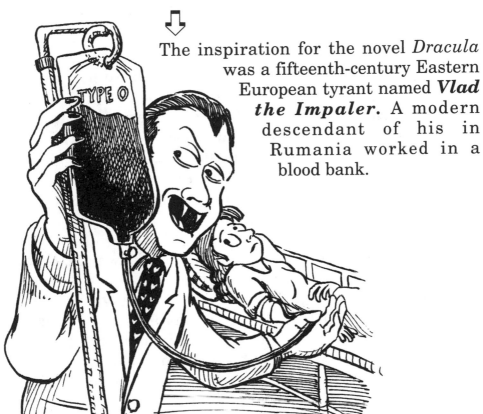

The inspiration for the novel *Dracula* was a fifteenth-century Eastern European tyrant named **Vlad the Impaler.** A modern descendant of his in Rumania worked in a blood bank.

⇨ In 1837, the unfinished novel *Narrative of Arthur Gordon Pym*, by **Edgar Allan Poe**, was published. It tells of four shipwrecked sailors who drew straws to see which would die so that the others might survive by eating his body. The cabin boy, Richard Parker, lost.

In 1884, three men stood trial for murder. They were the

actual survivors of a shipwreck. With one other person, they had drawn straws to see who would be killed and eaten so that the others might survive. The loser was the cabin boy. His name? Richard Parker.

❦

On May 3, 1812,
a British man tossed and turned
in his sleep as he dreamed of the violent
death of a British politician. The endangered
man in the dream was **Perceval Spencer,** then
prime minister of England. Eight days later, it all
came true. The dreamer had described the clothes
of the victim and of the attacker—Spencer in blue,
the attacker in brown—and it was so. In addition,
Spencer was shot to death exactly where
the dreamer had predicted—in the lobby
of the House of Commons.

❦

⇨ Charles Coughlan was born on Prince Edward Island in eastern Canada. In 1899, he died of a fever in Galveston, Texas, and was buried there. A **great hurricane** destroyed much of Galveston in 1900. Strange waves scoured coffins from their graves. Coughlan's coffin drifted out to sea. It was recovered by a fishing boat in 1908, just off the coast of Prince Edward Island . . . no more than a mile from where Coughlan had been christened as an infant.

# THE
# STILL MISSING
# MISSING LINK

The human family tree has been traced back to a point more than 1.5 million years ago. The chain, however, is broken. One of the great quests in science is to find the missing link that unites humans with their distant ancestors. Perhaps that is why, in 1912, so many reputable scientists were duped by one of the greatest hoaxes in history . . . the discovery of what is called the Piltdown man.

The tale began when a few teeth, some scraps of bone, and several simple stone tools called flints were unearthed from a gravel pit in East Sussex, England. The discoverer, an amateur archaeologist named Charles Dawson, was thrilled. He was certain that the humble find was in fact quite spectacular. He consulted Arthur Woodward, a colleague at the British Museum. Woodward agreed that this was an important find, and he soon joined Dawson in his excavation. Shortly afterward, at the same spot, they carefully extracted a large segment of a jawbone from the dark soil. Although the bone appeared to be that of an ape, its teeth were worn down in a pattern unique to humans. Was it possible the bone *was* of a human ancestor? Had the men found the long-sought missing link?

The scientific world responded enthusiastically. Since the fossils had been uncovered in a place called Piltdown Common, the creature was called Piltdown man. Many other fossils were found in the area as well, including more tools and the bones of ancient rhinos, elephants, and beavers. When the human-like bone fragments were studied, it appeared that they were part of a large, thick skull. The jawbone was broken and so could not be matched to the skull, but to what else could the jawbone possibly belong? Here, at last, was the half-man, half-ape that science had been searching for.

Further tests showed that the jaw was actually that of a young female who was generally a plant eater and did not yet have the power of human speech. Some investigators placed the bone fragments at about 500,000 years old, which, at the time, made them the oldest human fossils yet discovered. Dawson and his associates became quite famous. Many more fossils were uncovered in the area and nearby, including material from what might have been a second individual.

But, as wonderful as Piltdown man seemed to be, not everyone was completely convinced. A scientist from King's College in England noted that the jaw was suspiciously similar to that of a chimpanzee. The teeth, he pointed out, looked as though they might have been

The term *canard* is used to mean a ridiculous hoax. The usage stems from a nineteenth-century experiment that was supposedly carried out using 20 ducks. The hoaxer reported that he had killed one of the ducks and fed it to its fellow ducks. He continued the same claim each day until only one duck was left. For some reason, this caught the fancy of the press and so received a lot of coverage. It was, however, just a prank (no such experiment ever took place). Since then, a silly hoax has been called a canard . . . the French word for "duck."

purposely altered. The critics were few, though. When Charles Dawson died in 1916, the world mourned an important scientist.

It was not until 1949, when more accurate tests were available, that the hoax began to unravel. One chemical test in particular brought the age of the jawbone much nearer to 50,000 years than 500,000. Now that doubts had been raised, other scientists became involved. By 1953, it had been proved that although the skull fragments were human, the jaw belonged to a young female orangutan. The teeth had been filed to show the sort of wear typical of

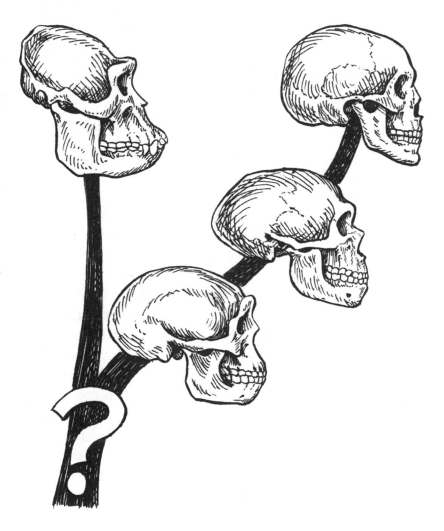

**In 1871,**
*a fire destroyed much of downtown Chicago. That fire has been blamed on a* **cow** *that supposedly kicked over a lantern in a straw-filled barn. The cow was said to belong to a Mrs. O'Leary. Although the origin of the fire was indeed traced to that woman's residence, it is more likely that a* **clumsy human** *began the blaze. Reporter Michael Ahern admitted to making up the cow story.*

human teeth. The bone had been chemically stained to match the soil of the gravel pit at Piltdown Common. Rather than being one of the greatest archaeological finds, Piltdown man was a very clever fake that had deceived the entire scientific community for years. Further investigation showed that the animal fossils found in the area were also suspect. Some had come from as far away as the Mediterranean.

Whoever had engineered the hoax was extremely knowledgeable about fossils and human anatomy. Most people suspected Charles Dawson. The find had brought him the fame he had always wanted. There is, however, another possibility. Near the site in East Sussex lived a man who was known for his interest and expertise in the subject of archaeology. He was said to love a good hoax, and he had reason to want to embarrass those in the scientific community—being an amateur archaeologist, they had disregarded many of his ideas. The man, who knew Dawson and often visited the site, was quite capable of concocting a very complex but believable tale. He had done just that for his most famous character …Sherlock Holmes. The man was Sir Arthur Conan Doyle.

Still, no one is really sure who engineered the deception. That is the true mystery of Piltdown man.

# THE  WHO NEVER EXISTED

Sometimes a hoax may be invented for a good cause. That was the case of a World War II charade that may have saved many thousands of lives. In 1942, it became necessary to convince the German and Italian forces that Sicily, the large island at the toe of boot-shaped Italy, would *not* be the landing site of an Allied invasion. This was important because, due to its strategic location, Sicily was an obvious target, and, in fact, it was precisely where the British planned to come ashore.

The trick was to get false documents into the hands of the enemy. And the plan was to have the documents delivered by a dead man! The general idea was to plant false papers on a body and allow it to be "discovered." Royal Naval Intelligence located the body of a man who had recently died of pneumonia. The family permitted the body to be used for the ruse for the good of the nation. The man was given a new identity, that of a Royal Marine named Major William Martin. Identification papers were quickly produced to make the trick believable. The heart of the hoax was a "top secret"

★

*During World War II, Hermann Goering, a member of the German high command, purchased a very expensive painting from a Dutch art dealer named Van Meegeren. Goering paid the man with counterfeit money. He got what he paid for. The painting, purportedly signed by the famous artist Vermeer, was a forgery that had actually been painted by Van Meegeren.*

★

29

document in a briefcase chained to the man's wrist. It cleverly and inaccurately informed a member of the British high command that the invasion would be directed at the island of Sardinia, far to the west of Sicily.

The problem of getting the papers into the hands of the Germans was readily solved. Because "Major Martin" had died of pneumonia, his body could be mistaken for that of a drowning victim (the effects on human lungs are similar in pneumonia and in drowning), one who had perhaps been a passenger in a plane that had crashed at sea. The body was taken aboard the British submarine Seraph, then under cover of darkness, it was set adrift in the sea off the coast of Spain. Although Spain was neutral in the conflict, the

Allies were certain that German spies would see the documents.

Shortly afterward, the British were advised that a Spanish fisherman had discovered the body of a Royal Marine. He was given a proper burial, and a few days later his belongings—including the false documents—were returned. The trick had worked: the folder that held the top secret material had been tampered with.

When, on September 3, 1943, the British 8th Army landed at Sicily, there was little armed resistance present. The German troops had been concentrated at Sardinia. The Italian government surrendered to the Allies within just five days, and a little more than a month later it declared war on its former ally, Germany.

The cost in human lives in securing the surrender of Italy was terribly high, but many believed that thousands of others had been spared because of Major William Martin—a man who never existed.

A golden tiara held a place of honor at the Louvre Museum in Paris for seven years. It was thought to be 2,200 years old. Eventually, a man who had actually made the tiara as a hoax came forward and confessed. The crown was quietly removed from its display.

# The Curse of the MUMMY'S TOMB

In January 1749, a British newspaper carried an *amazing advertisement.* The ad boasted of a performer who claimed he could crawl into a wine bottle and sing while witnesses actually picked up the bottle and inspected it. The ad was meant to be absurd. It had been placed as part of a bet between two noblemen. One of the men asserted that you could draw a crowd to such an event no matter how ridiculous it sounded. He was proved correct: the event was a sellout.

In 1922, British archaeologist Howard Carter finally realized a dream that had obsessed him for 25 years—the discovery of King Tut's tomb. On November 6, Carter stood in front of a stone door in Egypt's Valley of the Kings. It was a door that had been sealed for more than three thousand years. Behind it lay the treasures and the mortal remains of Tutankhamen, the boy king of ancient Egypt. As excited as Carter was to simply find the door, before opening and entering the tomb the archaeologist first contacted his friend and benefactor Lord Carnarvon to tell him the wonderful news. Carnarvon arrived from England as quickly as possible. With the help of several workers, they broke through the door, only to discover another one not far beyond.

Carter began work on the second stone door by chipping a small opening in it. Then he shined his flashlight in and gasped. The inner room was filled with gold and precious stones that had not seen the sun for 30 centuries. One of the world's greatest archaeological discoveries, the entire tomb was made up of four rooms, each filled with its own riches. The mummy of the boy king—who had become pharaoh when he was only 8 or 9 years old and then died at the age of 18—rested in a coffin of pure gold.

Word of the find spread around the world. Everyone was fascinated. In the capitals of Europe, fashion trends were launched to honor the pharaoh, and everything Egyptian was suddenly all the rage. The story was marvelous enough on its own merit, but certain reporters chose to expand upon it. One journalist in particular admitted to inventing an interesting and exciting story that was nothing but a hoax intended to help sell papers. He falsely wrote that there had been an inscription over the door of the tomb—an inscription that supposedly threatened death to all who entered it. Although it was untrue, the fanciful story caught the public's imagination.

When Lord Carnarvon died five months later in Cairo, the rumor took on a life of its own. Two Egyptian brothers involved in the find met violent ends. One was murdered in his hotel room, and the other supposedly committed suicide. An American who had complained of catching cold in the ancient tomb passed away from pneumonia—the same condition that had claimed Lord Carnarvon.

Finally, Carnarvon's half-brother joined the roll call of fatalities, bringing the list to a total of 12 people. Whether such an inscription truly existed or not, believers in the mummy's curse said that the deaths were far from coincidental.

Those who scoffed at the curse pointed out that the deaths were unrelated. In fact, Howard Carter himself, the first to gaze on the pharaoh's tomb, lived 17 more years, then died of natural causes at 66. There is, however, a postscript. In 1966, the contents of the tomb were sent on tour to Europe. The man who was the Egyptian director of antiquities at the time felt very strongly that something would go wrong. He sensed that he should keep the pharaoh in Egypt, but he was finally overruled. Two days later, he was killed in a car accident. Was the mummy's curse reaching out to punish him for his failure . . . or was it just one more strange coincidence that has helped to perpetuate one newspaper reporter's hoax?

# A Hoax OR Two OR More

The ***Cardiff Giant*** was discovered in 1869 by two men digging a pit on a New York farm. At first, some people thought the huge, 10-foot-tall statue pulled from the earth was a petrified man. Others believed it was a centuries-old image carved by an artisan of some long-forgotten race. William Newell, the farmer who owned the land on which the discovery was made, profited greatly by allowing people to see the marvel at 50 cents per viewing. Eventually, it became obvious that the whole thing was a hoax crafted by Newell and his brother-in-law, George Hull. Strangely, people then became even more curious about the fake that had tricked many experts. Newell continued to display the giant, and profits continued to pour in.

Have you ever tried to play a trick on your friends or family by disguising yourself? Perhaps the greatest ruse of all time was played in 1910, by a British trickster and his famous accomplices. **William Cole** loved to play practical jokes. His friends eventually became wise to him and seldom fell prey. That was when he decided to fool no less then Her Majesty's Royal Navy! A group of his pals put on makeup and special costumes and pawned themselves off as visiting Eastern princes, with Cole posing as their guide. They were given a royal welcome and a special tour of the Navy's most prized battleship. Among the hoaxsters was the famous British author Virginia Woolf.

*In* the early 1900s, a *racehorse owner* hoped to fix the results of a particular race in Belgium. Through his careful planning, every horse entered happened to belong to him. He secretly instructed each of the riders about the order in which the horses were to cross the finish line. A foolproof scheme? Not in this case. It seems that nature had a few tricks of her own up her sleeve. During the contest, a dense fog rolled in. The riders could not see one another and so could not keep track of the order in which they crossed the finish line. The hoax was a failure.

❋

# THE LONG ARM OF THE LAW

In 1935, a large shark was caught in Australian waters and transferred to a local sea aquarium. During a severe bout of indigestion, the shark emptied its stomach, and out drifted a human arm. Although some tooth marks marked the flesh, it was found that the arm had been severed not by a shark's teeth, but by a knife. The bizarre murder investigation that followed is officially referred to as the Shark Arm Case.

The 14-foot-long shark had been captured off Australia's Coogee Beach on April 17. It was a tiger shark, a powerful species known to occasionally attack humans. The fisherman's brother, Charles Hobson, felt the animal would make a first-rate addition to his sea aquarium. For a few days, all went well. When the fish grew sluggish and refused to eat, Hobson became concerned that it might not survive. By the end of the week the shark had belched up the entire contents of its stomach. Onlookers were stunned to see the ghastly pale flesh of a human arm float slowly to the bottom of the tank, with a short piece of rope tied at the wrist.

Hobson immediately called the police. The shark circled as Constable John Mannion and Detective Frank Head removed the arm from the water. They took fingerprints and were later able to identify the victim as James Smith. He was a man who had had several run-ins with the law, and his fingerprints were on file. A tattoo on the upper portion of the gruesome arm confirmed the identification.

The officers interviewed the man's family and were told that he had been gone since April 8, but they had believed he was on a fishing trip with a friend. Smith's wife, Gladys, had not been concerned at first, because on April 13 she had received a message. A neighbor said that James had called and would not be back as early as he had planned. Still, she did find it odd that he had not called her directly. It was not until April 24 that she began to be alarmed. She contacted the man who had supposedly accompanied her husband on the fishing trip, only to find out that no such trip had been scheduled.

The distraught woman was taken to the morgue, where she confirmed that the arm had come from her husband's body. Not long after, a friend of Smith's was arrested and brought to trial for the murder. The case could not be proved, and the man was acquitted. His defense

A man in Charleston, South Carolina, planned to pull an after-hours bank heist. He wrote out a demand for money and slipped it into the automatic teller machine. When the machine didn't respond, he shot it.

▲

*In ancient China, public drunkenness was once punishable by death by strangulation.*

▼

was simple: The police had an arm, but that was all— and since it was certainly possible for a man to lose an arm and still survive, the supposed murder victim might be very much alive! The rest of James Smith's body was never recovered. To this day, the Shark Arm Case remains unsolved.

# The Curse of the Idol's Eye

The history of the Hope diamond is uncertain, but it is thought to have begun in 1642 with a daring theft. Since then, its legacy has been an unfortunate trail of crime and disaster. The breathtaking sapphire-blue gem may have been cut from a much larger stone of more than 112 carats (roughly the size of a Ping-Pong ball). The diamond served as the eye of an Indian idol. It was pried from its place by a Hindu priest and sold to a French adventurer named Jean Baptiste Tavernier, who eventually sold it to King Louis XIV of France. Later, both the priest and Tavernier met ghastly fates (with Tavernier reputed to have been torn apart by wild dogs).

To improve the diamond's brilliance, the king had the fabulous diamond recut to a 67-carat, drop-shaped gem. The stone, which came to be known as the French Blue, seemed to bring disaster to anyone who touched it. A trusted government official who borrowed it was soon convicted of embezzlement and died in prison. Louis XIV himself ended his days in disgrace. The necklace was eventually passed on to Louis XVI and his wife,

Marie Antoinette, who occasionally wore it around her neck. During the French Revolution, that neck was separated from its royal head by the sharp blade of a guillotine. The Princess de Lambelle, a close friend to the queen, wore the jewel often. Her life ended when she was beaten to death by an angry mob, also during the French Revolution.

The French Blue disappeared for a number of years, finally resurfacing in London as a smaller, cushion-shaped gem of 44.5 carats. Rumors spread that the British sea captain responsible for transporting it across the English Channel committed suicide. The jeweler thought to have cut the stone suffered a heart attack shortly afterward.

British banker Thomas Hope (whose name became associated with the diamond) scoffed at the stories and purchased the jewel. His family fortunes declined rapidly, and the stone was sold to raise cash. Over the next 16 years, several owners of the Hope diamond were brought to ruin or even death, and crimes associated with the stone mounted. In 1908, a Turkish sultan gave the diamond as a gift to his lady love. A year later, he stabbed her to death and lost his throne. A Russian prince gave the necklace to an actress, also as a symbol of his love. The following year he shot her during a stage performance. The next victim was killed in a carriage accident, along with his wife and child.

In 1955, a Parisian man killed his wife during an argument over an undercooked meal. Seventeen years later he killed his second wife in an argument over an overcooked roast. Another Parisian man was arrested for stabbing his wife to death with a large wedge of Parmesan cheese.

Edward McLean, then owner of the *Washington Post* newspaper, purchased the Hope in 1911. The McLean family suffered many tragedies: One son died in a car crash, a daughter died of a drug overdose, and McLean himself died in an insane asylum. Nevertheless, Mrs. McLean did not believe in the legendary curse. The diamond remained in the family until her death in 1947. Harry Winston, an American diamond merchant, then acquired the Hope diamond and presented it to the Smithsonian Institution in Washington, D.C., making it the property of the American people.

Is the curse of the Hope diamond merely an imaginative story helped along by coincidence? Let's hope so.

# THE SALE
## — OF THE —
# CENTURY

The Eiffel Tower stands near the Seine River in Paris. A well-known landmark of that lovely city, the 984-foot-tall iron tower was built in 1889, and today it ranks among the most popular tourist attractions on the planet. It seems unlikely that the French government would put the monument up for sale, but in the early 1900s a pair of con men convinced a Parisian businessman of exactly that.

*Many banks supply blank deposit slips for their customers. An employee in a Boston bank once replaced all of the slips with new ones ...imprinted with the employee's own account number.*

One of the two con men was a Belgian named Victor Lustig, who presented himself as an official of France's ministry of public buildings. An American, Dan Collins, posed as his secretary. They set up the scheme carefully and chose their victims well. Collins contacted five French businessmen who dealt in scrap iron. The men were told that the Eiffel Tower was too costly to maintain and that it was to be torn down and scrapped. The men were asked to submit sealed bids for the valuable iron. They were instructed not to mention the deal to others, for various reasons.

The highest bid (the exact amount is unknown) was presented by Andre Poisson, who brought Lustig and Collins a certified check for the full amount. In exchange for this, he was given a bill of sale that confirmed his ownership of the tower.

Within an hour, the swindlers had cashed the check and were on their way out of the country. Strangely, the crime went unreported. Embarrassed by his gullibility, Poisson chose to keep quiet. The lack of publicity emboldened Lustig and Collins. They returned to Paris to try the deception again. Their next victim was more cautious and informed the police before any money changed hands. However, the lawbreakers managed to escape arrest.

A crime of this sort may seem too outrageous to be common . . . but this is not the case. Other landmarks and public monuments have been "sold" to unwary customers. An Englishman by the name of Arthur Furguson was particularly good at this scam. In various deals during the 1920s he sold London's Big Ben, Nelson's Column (a monument to Admiral Lord Nelson in Trafalgar Square), and Buckingham Palace (the ancestral home of the queen), for a

total of about 45,000 American dollars. It must have created quite a stir when the "new owner" tried to move into the royal abode!

The scheming con artist didn't stop there. Soon after moving to the United States, Furguson secured a tidy sum for a 99-year lease on the White House! He was just wrapping up the sale of the Statue of Liberty when his buyer became suspicious. Furguson had explained to the man that the city fathers planned to widen New York Harbor, and they simply had no place to put the cumbersome statue. Perhaps that sounded reasonable at first, but when the time came to close the deal, it was the police, not the intended victim, who met Furguson.

Furguson spent five years in prison and then moved to Los Angeles, California, to live out the rest of his life. There is no record that he conducted any further "business deals"—but if you happen to come across a deed to Grauman's (now Mann's) Chinese Theater or the Hollywood Walk of Fame, you'll know where it probably came from.

**IN 1786,** a Frenchman was sentenced to 50 years in prison for whistling at the French queen, Marie Antoinette.

■   ■   ■

The occurrence of most crimes rises dramatically when there is a **FULL MOON.** Murder, however, is one of the few crimes that does not seem to be affected.

# More SLIMY Crimes

☞ The spark that ignited World War I in 1914 was a ***brutal murder.*** Archduke Francis Ferdinand of Austria and his wife were assassinated while riding in their car. The convertible in which the couple was riding went on to claim a few victims of its own. Of the seven or so people who owned it after the crime, six were either killed or maimed in car accidents or were involved in car accidents that caused the deaths of others. The seventh committed suicide.

> ♣
>
> In 1942, a man was put on trial for trying to smuggle extremely valuable postage stamps out of France. Authorities claimed that he was attempting to avoid paying the costly export duties. In order to prove his innocence, the accused had to admit to another crime. He had forged the stamps and they were, in fact, worthless. For the crime for which he was brought to trial—he was found not guilty.
>
> ♣

☞ The ***murder*** of 13 crew members of a military transport plane in 1939 has never been solved. The plane was on a routine flight from San Diego to Honolulu. At one point, the base received a short distress call from the pilot, but then the radio went dead. The plane was landed by the fatally wounded copilot, who died within minutes without shedding any light on the mystery. The other 12 crewmen were already dead. All had large, open wounds, and the outside of the craft had been badly damaged, as if it had been battered by some sort of weapon. The first of the ground crew to enter the stricken plane noticed an odd, unidentifiable odor within, and investigators noted that both pilot and copilot had emptied their revolvers at something . . . but what? There was no sign of any other living thing aboard.

☞ In 1986, a Massachusetts **bank robber** failed in an attempt to get away from the scene of the crime. He had locked his keys in his car. A man in Oregon had similar difficulties when he tried to rob a convenience store. He left the keys to his getaway vehicle on the store counter. When he returned for them, he was apprehended. Probably the greatest insult was that to a Connecticut bank robber. While he was inside committing his crime, his getaway car was stolen.

# SLIME TIME

In the early days of science-fiction movies, a film premiered featuring a strange, slimy blob of goo as the monster. The "star" of *The Blob* arrived as a mere handful of celestial glop that coasted to earth in a meteor, grew to tremendous proportions, and soon terrorized the countryside. Imagine a wave of slime creeping slowly forward, flowing over or around every living thing in its path!

On a much smaller scale, the role the fictional blob filled is already taken by a terrestrial form of life . . . the slime mold. This unusual life-form has characteristics of both fungi and simple animals. It belongs to a special kingdom of living things called Protista, which includes algae as well as a hodgepodge of other odd forms.

Slime molds may dwell in the damp mat of the forest floor or deep inside rotting logs. Each begins as a single cell. In a very soggy or wet environment, the developing cell becomes a swarm cell, which is ringed with hair-like structures known as flagella (fluh-JEL-uh). The flagella act as tiny propellers, moving the cell from place to place. Cells that settle in a merely damp environment become myxamoeba (mik-suh-MEE-buh). They lose their flagella but are able to creep along without them. The cell isn't stuck with this arrangement, however. If conditions change, the slime mold is able to transform itself by developing or absorbing flagella in a matter of moments. If things become really unbearable (that is, too dry), it secretes a special, durable cell wall and patiently waits out the bad times.

Slime molds feed on bacteria and other organic matter by flowing around and then absorbing them. (Who feeds on slime molds? Worms, of course.)

When temperature and moisture conditions are just right, the slime mold cells collect in a slippery blob and ooze toward the surface of a log or soil to reach the light. Since they are unable to survive when exposed to direct sunlight, they form a slick mass on the shadowy undersides of rotting logs or in damp leaf litter.

The mass, called the plasmodium (plaz-MOHD-ee-um), usually resembles a lacy fan with ruffled edges. The typical color is yellow, though pink or red is not uncommon. At this stage, some plasmodia are so

The penguin is the only bird that molts (sheds) all of its feathers at one time.

Nine-banded armadillos always give birth to four identical young.

small that they are invisible to the naked eye. Others may cover an area that is several yards across. (One scientist reportedly grew a "pet" slime mold that covered his basement floor!) The gooey plasmodium creeps slowly along, squeezing through tiny cracks and openings. It may harden into a special form to resist an unfavorable environment, then return to prime slime when the weather improves.

After the plasmodium has developed, the gooey blobs develop flowerlike bodies called sporophores (SPOR-uh-forz), which have remarkable colors and shapes. The sporophores may appear as red cotton-candy puffs, golden hairlike mats, thin strands that resemble pink coral, or glimmering purple beads. The largest are no more than an inch tall, and some are so small they can be seen only through a microscope.

The sporophores produce and release spores. Dispersed by rain, wind, or passing animals, each spore contains a living cell that will form a new swarm cell. So, if you get a chance to see the film *The Blob*, remember: Hollywood's version may be bigger, but nature thought of it first!

# BOMBS AWAY!

Many varieties of tools or weapons that humans have devised have already been put to use by animals. For example, when searching for warm-blooded prey, rattlesnakes use their remarkable heat-sensing capabilities. (Humans have developed infrared-sensitive satellites that detect heat sources at night.) Bats employ a form of radar to navigate and to locate food, and whales and dolphins use sonar to do the same. The electric eel produces an electrical field that aids in navigation and can be used to give an enemy a nasty jolt. Some animals, such as certain snakes and spiders, defend themselves by injecting venom into their attackers. Others even resort to "chemical warfare." Among the most effective of these is a small, ground-dwelling insect known as the bombardier beetle.

This aggressive little creature is found throughout much of the world, particularly in mild to tropical climates. There are 40 different varieties in the United States alone. Bombardier beetles range in length from less than a quarter of an inch to more than two inches. They live in a wide variety of habitats, but the largest of these creatures roam the rain

*The female anglerfish* may be as much as 20 times larger and a thousand times heavier than the male. But the tiny male has the truly strange habit of attaching himself to the body of the female and feeding directly from her bloodstream!

forests and grasslands of Africa and Asia. The bombardier beetle usually preys on small insects. In fact, many varieties begin their predatory behavior the moment they hatch. For example, the larva (the stage after the egg) of one North American bombardier beetle bores into the pupa (the stage following the larva stage) of a certain type of water beetle. There, the larva feeds on and eventually kills the helpless host.

By the time a bombardier beetle reaches adulthood, it has developed a most unusual defensive weapon: a harsh, hot spray of liquid that it can direct at its enemies, such as birds, lizards, or snakes. The liquid is created and stored in a pair of glands in the end of the animal's abdomen. These are called the pygidial (pih-JID-ee-ul) glands. Within these structures, special cells produce several chemical components, which are then stored in a tiny, muscular reservoir.

When the beetle must defend itself, a muscle in the reservoir relaxes, allowing the chemicals to pass into a combustion chamber. (The strong walls of this chamber are chemical- and heat-resistant.) At the same time, special enzymes are also released into the chamber. The enzymes cause the chemicals from the reservoir to combine, and so create a mini-explosion within the insect! The reaction causes harsh quinones, water, and oxygen to build up and finally blast explosively out through two small openings at the end of the creature's abdomen. Sometimes the explosion makes a sharp popping sound. The pressure in the chamber also heats the corrosive spray to nearly 212 degrees Fahrenheit! The entire process takes only a fraction of a second, and a bombardier beetle is capable of ejecting a series of as many as 20 foul-smelling blasts in a row. The remarkable insect is also able to aim its weapon quite accurately—and in any direction it likes!

Even large bombardier beetles are rarely harmful to humans. While their weapon may discharge if the insects are handled, the hot spray causes only a warm feeling when it comes in contact with human skin. The fluid will, however, stain skin, and it cannot be washed off. In fact, the dark, brownish blotch takes up to two or three weeks to completely wear away.

# THE WONDER DOWN UNDER

CERTAIN
MUSEUMS
use meat-eating
insects known as
carrion beetles to
clean bones.

THE YOUNG
of the air-breathing
hippopotamus are
generally born
under water. And
the young of the
water-dwelling giant
manta ray (a kind of
fish) may be born in
the air as the moth-
er leaps out of the
water.

"It's a hoax!" That was the general opinion of many Europeans when they were shown the body of a duckbill platypus in 1798. The unusual Australian mammal was thought to be a combination of different animals sewn together, including an otter and a duck. This astonishing creature *does* look a little like something that Mother Nature put together with a few odds and ends.

The platypus is a monotreme (MAHN-uh-treem), or egg-laying mammal. It shares that trait with only one other type of mammal, its prickly neighbor the echidna (ih-KID-nuh). Comfortable both on land and in water, the platypus is found throughout the freshwater rivers and lakes of eastern Australia and Tasmania. There, it searches for tadpoles, crayfish, water snails, and worms to eat, which it nuzzles out of the mud with its sensitive, pliable beak. Two horny spurs in the creature's upper and lower jaws, as well as a pair of horny "teeth" on the tongue, are perfect for crushing food.

An excellent swimmer, the platypus is

well-suited for aquatic life. It has a flattened tail for maneuvering under water, a dense, water-resistant coat, and protective flaps of skin over its eyes and ears. It powers itself through the water with its strong, webbed feet, using its back legs as rudders for steering and stabilizing. When on land, the platypus tucks the webbing of its feet under. This enables it to use its long claws for digging and burrowing.

Not surprisingly, the platypus also has strange nest-building habits. Instead of nesting comfortably above ground, or even digging an easy-access burrow, the female digs a tunnel in a riverbank. She claws her way through the mud and dirt, holding her breath with each step, until finally she has dug a tunnel that's 15 to 30 feet in length. Some tunnels may be as long as 100 feet. The animal then carves out a chamber at one end of the tunnel and lines it with grass, which she has gathered and carried back to the

Tailor ants come by their name honestly. To create their nests, adults *"sew"* the edges of leaves together by pushing their *larvae* through the leaves, just as if the larvae were needles. And the thread? It is *silk* spun by the larvae.

In an area of Germany known as the Tyrol, there is a superstition that wearing a *bat's left eye* over your own will make you *invisible.* Perhaps the truth of the matter is that the practice is so *repulsive* that no one would want to look at you!

nest by tucking it under her tail. Once the nest is completed, she lays one to three round eggs in the small alcove and incubates them for up to 12 days.

The hairless babies are less than an inch long when they hatch. They spend the next 17 weeks or so in the safety of the nest, until they reach a length of about 12 inches. Their mother feeds them milk produced in her mammary glands. The glands simply release the milk onto her skin, and the youngsters lap it up. Oddly, the young are born with teeth—as many as 12 in the upper jaw and 22 in the lower jaw. These are eventually lost and replaced by horny plates in the bill.

The duckbill platypus is not a very large animal. Males may reach 24 inches in length, with 6-inch-long tails. Females generally do not exceed 20 inches in length, and their tails are slightly shorter than those of the males. The average weight of a male platypus is only about four pounds. Still, the male is territorial and aggressive, and it has an interesting weapon to rely on. The platypus is one of the few mammals that is venomous. Nestled at the base of each rear foot is a sharp, hollow spur that is connected to a venom gland. The spur is used in fights with rivals, and the venom is potent enough to kill a large adult dog. The platypus may look comical, but its ability to protect itself is no joke!

# Is That WEIRD or What?

▲ The *mayfly* generally lives for only two hours. During that time, the insect's only goal is to mate. Since it has no need to eat, the mayfly is born without a mouth.

▲ The six-inch-long *hero shrew* of Africa has a most unusual backbone. Unlike that of other mammals, the spinal column of this little creature is a network of interlocking, bony rods that branch out from the vertebrae. This frame is so strong that a human could balance on the back of the hero shrew for several minutes without hurting the animal!

▲ The *world's largest bird,* the ostrich may tower up to 9 feet tall. The smallest bird, the 2½-inch bee hummingbird, is no larger than the eye of an ostrich.

▲ The *hagfish* is a very primitive, eel-like fish with no bones, jaws, or teeth. It produces a protective covering of slime that lubricates its skin. It is said that if you place one of these fish in a bucket of seawater, the bucket will quickly be filled with the thick, oozing slime. The hagfish usually feeds on dead or dying fish. It uses its raspy tongue to bore through the outer flesh, then sucks out its meal. For better leverage, the hagfish actually ties its long, thin body into a knot and presses up against its prey.

▲ Male *Magellan flightless steamer ducks* may not be able to fly, but, using their large webbed feet, the ducks can power themselves across the water at speeds of up to 25 miles per hour. This makes them the world's fastest surface-swimming bird.

▲ In 1837, a British soldier in Canada *saved a goose* from certain death in the jaws of a fox. It was not very long before the goose returned the favor by honking noisily and alerting that same guardsman to a sneak attack on his outpost by French Canadian rebels. Thus, the goose saved his friend and his regiment and became known as the "watch goose" of the Coldstream Guards.

▲ The *ground-dwelling mallee fowl* excavates a nest 2 to 3 feet deep and up to 10 feet in diameter. The birds construct the nest so precisely that they are able to maintain a constant temperature of 92 degrees Fahrenheit (plus or minus one degree) within the nest. Once the nest is complete, the male is the temperature-tester. By constantly probing the nest's walls with his heat-sensitive beak, he can tell whether material needs to be added or taken away from the nest.

▲ During the dry season, the *African lungfish* burrows into the mud at the bottom of a pool of water. Then it encases itself in mucus, which it produces itself. When the mucus dries, it forms a protective cocoon. In this way, if the pool dries up completely, the fish can survive for as long as four years in its special shelter.

▲ The *tadpole* of the paradoxical frog may be as much as 10 inches long, while the adult frog is barely more than 2 inches long. This very strange amphibian actually grows smaller as it grows older!

Now You See It, Now You Don't

# The Missing Prince

During the French Revolution in the late eighteenth century, hundreds of people met their deaths at the guillotine. Among those executed were the king and queen of France, Louis XVI and Marie Antoinette. The royal family of Bourbon did not end with the demise of Louis and Marie, however. Some family members were spared but imprisoned. Among those few survivors was the king and queen's son, Louis Charles. The young prince, or dauphin (doh-FAN), reportedly died in 1795 at the age of 10. But the report of his death was cloaked in mystery, and many challenged it. Countless people thought that the body buried in the coffin was not really his. Did the heir to the French throne and the family fortune survive?

The trail to discover what became of Louis Charles begins with the words of an elderly woman in a hospital in approximately 1815. "My little prince is not dead," she assured her nurse. That would have meant very little . . . *if* the old woman had not been the jailer of the dauphin until 1794, one year before he had supposedly died. She went on to confess that she and her husband had switched the young boy with a sickly orphan child of the streets, a child who soon passed away from his illness. The switch did not go unnoticed. The new jailer was convinced that his charge was an imposter, and others agreed.

Years later, the royal family of Bourbon was returned to its position as ruler of France. Dozens of men stepped forward, claiming to be the lost dauphin. One in particular, Karl Wilhelm Naundorff, bore an uncanny resemblance to the family. Several people who had known the young prince were convinced that he and Naundorff were one and the same. But the dauphin's sister, Therese, did not agree. Naundorff did not take the throne, and he died in Holland in 1842.

By 1846, more than half a century after the controversial body of a young boy had been buried, enough suspicion had been aroused that it was removed from its grave. Doctors determined that the bones were more likely those of an 18-year-old than of a 10-year-old child. The evidence in support of the prince's survival is tantalizing. But where he disappeared to and how he lived his life are nearly impossible questions to answer—unless the proof remains hidden somewhere, tucked away in a secret passage or locked in a vault . . . .

# FLIGHT 19: MYSTERIES OF THE BERMUDA TRIANGLE

*"Calling tower—this is an emergency. We seem to be off course. We cannot see land. Repeat: we cannot see land. . . ."*

These are the words of an unusual radio transmission that took place on December 5, 1945. The communication was between the leader of a squad of five Avenger torpedo bombers and the tower flight controller. The planes were on a routine patrol out of the Fort Lauderdale Naval Air Station in Florida. It was a mission that should have lasted only about two hours, but the 27 airmen of Flight 19 were never seen again. Their route took them deep into a region that has been the subject of controversy for many years. If you look at a map of the western Atlantic Ocean off the coast of Florida, imagine a triangle, the lines of which extend from Bermuda to Puerto Rico to Miami, then back to Bermuda. Roughly within those lines is an area of the sea that some say is harmless, but others fear. This area is known as the Bermuda Triangle.

Flight 19 took to the air at about 2:00 P.M. It was the last flight of a pleasant day, with clear weather. At 3:45, the unusual transmission above was received

In 1955, actor **JAMES DEAN** was killed in an accident while driving his **PORSCHE.** The car was badly damaged, but parts of it were sold. An amateur race-car driver bought the engine. During a race, his car went out of control and **CRASHED,** killing him. The body of the Porsche, while being moved by trailer to a new locale, was hit from behind by another car. The driver was thrown from the car and the Porsche slipped from its bonds, running over and killing the victim.

Eventually, the car was shipped to Los Angeles by train, but it **NEVER ARRIVED.** No one knows the final fate of the jinxed Porsche.

by the base operator. By that time the planes should have been within sight of the Florida coast.

The operator calmly responded to the nervous pilot, "What is your position?"

The reply was hesitant: "We're not sure of our position. We can't be sure where we are. We seem to be lost."

"Assume bearing due west," the operator advised.

"We don't know which way is west. . . . Everything is wrong . . . strange. Even the ocean doesn't look as it should."

The last transmission from the flight came at 4:25 P.M. "We are not certain where we are. . . . Think we must be about 225 miles northeast of base. . . . Looks like we are entering white water. We're completely lost."

A search plane was immediately sent out, but that craft, too, disappeared. Some believe an explosion might have occurred on the search plane about 20 minutes into its flight. What followed was the most tremendous air-and-sea search ever conducted in a rescue mission. Three hundred planes and ships were involved, over a period of five days. Not a

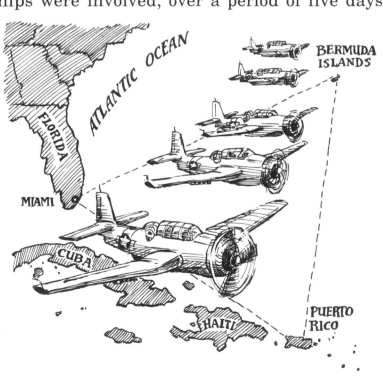

single clue or fragment of wreckage of the six missing planes was found.

Strange occurrences are not new to the region called the Bermuda Triangle. Christopher Columbus referred to an oddly luminous quality to the waters near the Bahamas. Even modern sailors and pilots have reported a luminous haze or glow in the atmosphere, as well as a shimmering in the sea as if lights had been turned on deep underwater.

To date, the count of unexplained disappearances is more than 60 ships and 40 planes. The count could be much higher, but in cases in which only debris was found, the ship was not counted. In several instances, the ships made it through, but the passengers did not. In 1940, a private boat called the *Rosalie* was discovered in excellent condition, but the only passengers were a cat, a chicken, and a canary.

But what of Flight 19? Some evidence suggests that the weather had taken a turn for the worse as the fateful day wore on. And, because of equipment failure, the pilots continued to change direction in an attempt to get their bearings. After four hours or so of wandering, the planes would have run out of fuel. Without knowing what really happened, we're left with the chilling words of one naval officer at the conclusion of the fruitless search for Flight 19: "They vanished as completely as if they had flown to Mars."

GALLIPOLI, *in Turkey, was the site of a famous World War I battle on August 28, 1915. As the battle was engaged, New Zealand soldiers reportedly witnessed at least 500 British soldiers advance into a loaf-shaped, low-lying cloud on the battlefield. The Britons did not exit the cloud, and when the fog lifted, they were completely gone.*

In 1939, Judge Joseph Crater, a Supreme Court justice of New York State, walked out of his hotel and *disappeared.* To this day he is still listed as missing. In 1959, a *psychic* was called in to give some possible insight. He claimed that the judge had been kidnapped and murdered and that his body would *never be found.* On a map, the psychic marked locations that had been critical to the case. None of the sites had been made public, so the man couldn't have previously known about them. So far, the psychic's prediction is *true*—the body has never been found.

# Not a Soul on Board

In the annals of strange disappearances, December 5 is most often remembered as the day that Flight 19 flew into the unknown (see p. 61). But on that same date 73 years earlier, a ship sailed *out* of the unknown. Her cargo was a mystery. She is known as the *Mary Celeste*.

On December 5, 1872, Captain Morehouse and the crew of the British ship *Dei Gratia* were sailing the Atlantic Ocean, heading on an easterly course for Gibraltar. It was early afternoon on a clear day, and the visibility was excellent. A sailor reported to the captain that a ship had been sighted in the distance, approaching on a direct westerly course. Captain Morehouse entered the information in his log, as was the routine. As the two vessels neared each other, however, it appeared that the sighting was far from routine. Morehouse went on to describe the ship in his log as having all but her main sails set, with some of the smaller sails in shreds. The slow-moving ship was progressing along an erratic course.

Those on the British ship could plainly see no one was steering the other craft. Why was she deserted, and what had happened to her crew? In the hope of discovering answers, three members of the

*Dei Gratia* crew boarded the strange vessel. However, all they uncovered was more questions. After searching thoroughly, they were confident that not a soul was aboard. It was noted that the lifeboat was, indeed, missing, but so was the tackle that would have been needed to lower it into the sea. And why would a crew abandon a perfectly sound vessel? There were no signs of violence or damage, and all of the possessions of the missing men were in place. If the ship had been abandoned, the sailors would certainly have taken some of those things with them. Thinking that the solution to the mystery might be in the ship's log, the searchers brought it back to the *Dei Gratia.*

The log showed that the ship was the American-owned *Mary Celeste*. The last entry had been made 10 days earlier on November 25, when the vessel was near a tiny island in the Azores known as Santa Maria (the Azores is a chain of islands in the Atlantic Ocean hundreds of miles from the coast of Spain). Captain Morehouse was startled. That meant that in 10 days and without crew, the *Mary Celeste* had sailed nearly 400 miles east (quite a distance for an abandoned ship), then turned and had begun sailing west again!

Captain Morehouse was determined to find out what had happened, especially after he discovered that the captain of the *Mary Celeste,* a man named Briggs,

**The *Mary Celeste*** had a history of misfortune. She was originally the *Amazon.* Her first captain died within two days of taking command. The ship then suffered a series of small accidents, including a collision with another ship. She was wrecked in Newfoundland in 1867 and left for anyone who wanted her. It was there that Captain Briggs recovered and renamed her.

*A group of British settlers landed on Roanoke Island in Virginia in 1587. When the ship returned to England, 10 men were left behind to establish a colony. When more colonists arrived, the original 10 were missing, gone without a trace. This time 100 were left behind, but the next ship found the island empty once again. The only clue left behind was the word* Croatan, *carved in a tree. That was the name of a nearby island. When it was searched, however, there was no sign of the settlers. There were no graves, and no indication of violence. Nothing has ever been found of them.*

was an acquaintance of his. In fact, they had dined together less than a month before. (Morehouse also remembered that Captain Briggs had planned to take his wife and young daughter with him when he next sailed.) Morehouse decided to put a small crew on the *Mary Celeste* and sail her to Gibraltar. She arrived in port one day after the *Dei Gratia*, on Friday, December 13.

An investigation concluded that the captain and his family had been killed by a mutinous crew, who had then abandoned the ship. Few people who knew the details of the case accepted that conclusion, however. There had been no evidence whatsoever of violence on board. Moreover, if the crew had abandoned ship, some would have taken their belongings, and there would probably have been signs of a hasty departure. Many small valuables were found on the craft, and its cargo of crude alcohol was undisturbed. Surely, that ruled out pirates. Also, there was no indication of bad weather. Everything in the ship's galley was neatly in place, and a vial of sewing-machine oil was found standing upright on a table. It was as if those aboard the ship had simply evaporated into thin air.

Over the past century, a number of theories have been presented to explain the puzzle, including everything from UFOs to sea monsters. A few people have even suggested that Captain Morehouse might have had something to do with the crew's disappearance, in a scheme to claim the ship as salvage.

What was the true fate of those on board the *Mary Celeste*? No clue to their fate has ever been uncovered. Aside from the log, only one other message was found aboard. It was the beginning of a letter from one ship's mate to his wife. It read, "Fanny, my dear wife, Frances M. R. . . . " There was no more. What had he wished to say to his wife? It is just one more part of the mystery that may forever shroud the *Mary Celeste*.

**?**

The ***Waratah*** was a brand-new ship weighing nine thousand tons. On April 27, 1909, she left England with 211 passengers and crew for a round-trip voyage to South Africa. Only one person on board would make it safely back. For three nights in a row and about midway to their first destination, passenger Claude Sawyer had a nightmare in which he saw a medieval knight in armor rise from the sea. Blood dripped from both the armor and the knight's upraised sword. Although it made no sound, he was sure the specter was saying *"Waratah."* At Durban, South Africa, Sawyer left the ship. The *Waratah* departed Durban, sailed into the void, and was

never heard from again. What happened to her is still a mystery.

More than two thousand years ago, Roman soldiers controlled parts of the British Isles. About 60 B.C., one large legion known as the *Unlucky Ninth* was the subject of a curse by Queen Boadicea of a British tribe. Some 60 years later, as four thousand or so soldiers of the Ninth marched toward Scotland, they disappeared. Their bodies were never found.

Although they were never seen again, the soldiers were reportedly heard as recently as the mid-twentieth century. Several residents of the town of Dunblane, Scotland, which lies on the very route taken by the legion, heard what sounded like an army marching—a huge army, since it took some 20 minutes to pass. No one saw a thing, but one couple reported that their dog and cat rose up growling and hissing and appeared to fearfully watch *something* go by for nearly half an hour.

**Fatal Fortunes**

# THE MONEY PIT

Some hidden treasure hoards are said to be protected by such obstacles as phantoms, or perhaps an ancient curse. The "money pit" of Oak Island, off Nova Scotia, needs no such supernatural guards. It is one of the most brilliant feats of engineering ever devised to hide bounty.

The origin of Oak Island's treasure is not certain. Pirates, perhaps . . . but there is another theory. The pit appears to have been dug at about the same time as the American Revolutionary War. It has been suggested that British soldiers sank the shaft (or pit) and used it as a safe hiding place for the pay chest destined for their New York military post. In that case, the pit would have been constructed by the British Royal Engineers, which could explain its remarkable nature.

The pit was discovered in 1795 by 16-year-old Daniel McGinnis. He and two friends had rowed to the island to hunt for small game. While searching for prey, they discovered a tackle box hanging from a tree. The weatherworn equipment was the kind that sailors used for handling bulky gear or cargo. Below the tree was a depression in the sand. The boys became curious and began to dig up the area. At first they ran into a layer of stones, which they removed. Then, at each 10-foot level (down to 30 feet) they found platforms made of oak.

Their report piqued the curiosity of treasure seekers. An expedition in 1804 discovered five more oak platforms. Some were sealed with ship's putty and with coconut fibers of a variety found in the South Seas. At 90 feet, the searchers brought up something quite different. It was a stone that has come to be called the Cypher Stone. It was covered with unusual symbols, which appeared to indicate the presence of "10 million buried 10 feet below." Feeling close to their prize, the workers dug deeper. One evening, as darkness fell, a man felt his shovel hit something very hard. Everyone agreed that it was a chest, but the rest of the digging was put off until the following day.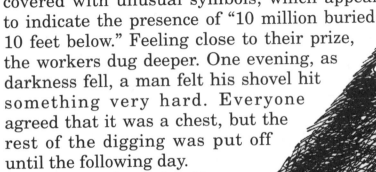

The dawn brought disappointment. Overnight, water had seeped into the pit and refilled it to the 60-foot level. Pumps and bailing buckets were useless. In another attempt to drain the pit, the laborers dug a tunnel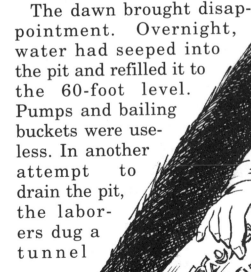

**LEGEND HAS IT**

*that two centuries ago, robbers hid $11 million in Spanish gold in a cave in what is now Oklahoma canyon country. The entrance to the cave is supposedly sealed by a huge iron door secured with a tremendous padlock. It may seem that an iron door would be easy to spot in a canyon wall, but it has supposedly rusted to the color of the brick-red earth.*

nearby, then tried to dig sideways, but water rose in the second pit as well. So close, and yet so far! Eventually, the team was forced to abandon hope.

In 1849, another group attempted to bring up the chest, but their efforts only weakened the shaft. It collapsed into what seemed to be a large cavern, 180 feet deep. During the excavation, the treasure seekers made an amazing discovery. They had known that the water level in the pit always rose and fell with the tide, and now they learned why. Whoever had built the shaft had also constructed side tunnels that led to the sea. One joined the pit at about 110 feet deep. In 1942, a second tunnel was found at 150 feet.

If the shaft was indeed dug by the British, they may have come back later and retrieved the chest, leaving the pit empty . . . but maybe not. Although little more than a few stray links of gold chain have ever been retrieved from the money pit, to this day searchers still risk life and limb and a great deal of hard cash to uncover the buried riches. A total of some $1.5 million has already been poured into the quest to probe the bottom of the pit. The search for hidden fortune can *cost* a fortune: the latest cost estimate for preparations to recover the legendary $10 million treasure of Oak Island is . . . $10 million.

# Treasure Island

What do you think of when you hear the words *buried treasure*? Perhaps images of pirates come to mind . . . or curious, faded maps scrawled on rolls of parchment . . . or chests filled with gleaming gold. The story of Cocos Island has all of these elements, and more. Named for the coconut palms that sway on its sandy shores, Cocos Island might easily be called Treasure Island. Near the west coast of Costa Rica, it was the well-documented hiding place of several notorious pirates from the seventeenth to the nineteenth centuries. There is a large body of evidence that a great deal of pirate wealth is buried somewhere on that uninhabited speck of land in the Pacific Ocean. Since the island is only five miles long by two and a half miles wide, it seems that nothing could remain hidden there for long. Still, Cocos Island has kept its secrets safe from dozens of hopeful treasure seekers.

The island itself is formed by three volcanic peaks and is covered with dense jungle. Lining the southern shore are steep cliffs, 600 feet high, that present a barrier to any ship. But to the north and east, two small waterways cut through

※
Statistically, it has been estimated that 10 years after a treasure has been buried, there is only a 50 percent chance that it will ever be found. As time passes, the odds grow much higher against recovery.
※

the jungle to the sea. It is there that small boats can make their way to the interior.

The first rumor of treasure surrounds a British buccaneer named Edward Davis. It is said that Davis and his men preyed upon wealth-filled Spanish galleons, then buried the spoils somewhere on the little island. Some say that the pirate retrieved his loot after being pardoned by King James II, but others claim the treasure is still hidden.

Another mysterious treasure connected to the island is that of the British ship the *Mary Dear*. The tale begins around 1820, when the *Mary Dear* was in port in Lima, Peru. At that time, the city was under Spanish rule and being threatened by rebels. To protect their tremendous wealth, the Spaniards secured the services of the *Mary Dear* to transport the treasure to safety. They loaded her with a fortune in gold and gems and set sail. The crew, however, had other plans. They murdered the Spanish guard and passengers and made off with the ship.

The pirate crew needed a place to put the loot, which was estimated at

about 16 tons of treasure. Their solution was Cocos Island.

The *Mary Dear* was eventually apprehended and her crew hanged, with the exception of two men who managed to escape. One soon died, but the second, a man identified as Thompson, survived. Years later, on his deathbed in Newfoundland, he revealed the treasure's hiding place to a friend named Keating, who supposedly recovered some of the treasure. However, it turned out to be such a grueling task that Keating decided not to even try for the rest. Much of the wealth on that tiny island remains unclaimed, but Keating left clues concerning landmarks, compass headings, and the number of paces to take at various points in the search. Some hints are mysterious and romantic, such as the instruction to stand at a certain spot near sunset. As the sun dips to the horizon, you must then wait for a rock that casts a shadow that resembles an eagle. The phantom bird points to an important cave that supposedly holds some treasure. In addition to Keating's clues, there exists a map that was reputedly drawn by a crew member of the *Mary Dear.*

In 1891, a German fortune seeker named Gissler actually moved to the desolate island. He remained there for 17 long years, eventually marrying and bringing his wife to live on the island. But they were rarely alone: treasure hunters arrived from all over the world

❖

*Native legends* tell of a time past when two great ships flew at each other like birds in battle. After much thunder and smoke, one ship sailed away and the other was washed ashore. The sailors dragged a huge *treasure chest* up onto the beach and buried it in a pit, but not before killing a man described as a *giant* and shoving his body into the same hole. Since then, the remains of an old sailing vessel and several skeletons have been discovered. One of the skeletons was that of a man nearly *eight feet tall.* No treasure, however, has yet been found.

❖

*P*IRATES HAVE CLAIMED THAT PIERCING ONE'S EAR AND WEARING A GOLD EARRING IMPROVED THEIR EYESIGHT. ODDLY, THE EARLOBE IS A SITE THAT ACUPUNCTURISTS USE TO TREAT EYE AILMENTS.

to try their hands at deciphering the cryptic leads. Gissler established a colony and was appointed governor of the island by the Costa Rican government. He found 33 gold coins, all in different locations, but that was the only success he had.

Gissler's lack of victory didn't discourage others. In 1897, an expedition of 300 British sailors and marines tried their luck at finding the booty. They left empty-handed, as future expeditions would do time after time—that is, until 1932, when the story takes a turn. A British explorer by the name of Colonel Leckie was said to have finally located a large cache of gold on the island. The government of Costa Rica sent soldiers to pursue a search of their own, and a part of the treasure was said to have been recovered. But if true, even though it was thought to be a great deal of gold, it was still only a small portion of the total riches rumored to be buried in the sands of Treasure Island.

# THE LOST DUTCHMAN'S MINE

Not all great treasures are hidden away on islands or at the bottom of the sea. The mountains in the vast Arizona desert conceal the location of what is thought to be a tremendous fortune in gold. The legend of the Lost Dutchman's Mine is one of treachery and great wealth in the American Southwest. Although several men have reaped benefits from the mine, it is rumored to bear a curse. Death and disaster seem to stalk all who attempt to claim it for their own.

The first mention of the mysterious mine is in Spanish accounts dating from 1748. Apache Indians supposedly revealed the treasure's locale to Spanish monks traveling north from Mexico. A somewhat suspicious record shows that the mine then became part of a land grant to Don Miguel Peralta from King Ferdinand of Spain. Although the Apaches allowed the Peralta family to take advantage of the mine for a time, they came to resent the presence of the intruders. In 1864, when family member Enrico Peralta took a small expedition to the area, he and his group were mysteriously killed. One man survived the battle

*Treasure* can be different things to different people. At one time, South American Indians who lived along the banks of the Amazon River used the dried flesh of a *large fish* called the arapaima as currency. Until a century ago, the *teeth of dogs* were currency on the Solomon Islands. Money on the Yap Islands of the South Pacific comes in the form of *18-foot-tall stone rings*. That gives new meaning to the phrase "small change"!

**Lake Guatavita,**
in Colombia, South
America, was once
the site of a bizarre
Indian ritual. The
chieftain would be
covered in gold dust
and rowed to the
center of the lake.
There, he would
dive in and rinse off
the gold.
Meanwhile, other
members of the
tribe would throw
gifts of gold and
emeralds into the
incredibly deep
body of water.
Modern prospectors
have attempted to
probe the depths of
Lake Guatavita, but
none have been
successful in their
quest for treasure.

and returned to Mexico with a map of what he vowed was the site of the mine. However, few outsiders were willing to risk their lives to enter the hazardous region.

In 1870, an Arizona man by the name of Abraham Thorne befriended his Apache neighbors. The Indians offered to take him to a place where, they said, he could gather up chunks of gold from the ground. They blindfolded Thorne and led him to a canyon that was unfamiliar to him. Thorne returned with $6,000 worth of precious nuggets that he had scooped into his pockets! But the taste for treasure proved to be his undoing. Thorne was able to retrace his steps, and when he returned to the mine with friends, they were all slain.

The next chapter in the story tells of two German men, Jacob Waltz and Jacob Weiser. The pair claimed that the son of Enrico Peralta had offered to take them to the mine as thanks for their having aided him in a fight. They returned from the site with 10 times the amount of Thorne's booty, then purchased the rights to the mine from Peralta. Surprisingly, they had little trouble with the Apaches at first. They worked the mine in peace, and all seemed well. But their luck didn't hold. Weiser suddenly disappeared, and all that Waltz found in camp were arrows and part of a bloody shirt. Weiser's fate was obvious. Waltz abandoned the mine.

When Jacob Waltz died, he left behind

no record of the mine's location. Although he and his partner had been German, people mistook Waltz's accent for Dutch and the lost treasure came to be known as the Lost Dutchman's Mine.

Before long, the Apaches, too, realized that the lure of gold meant too much trouble. They filled in the mine and toppled rock landmarks. A timely earthquake helped them in their task. One landmark that apparently remained in place was an unusual, sharp pinnacle of rock.

Many others tried to find the mine, based on vague reports of its whereabouts. In about 1881, two soldiers rode into a town thought to be near the mine. Their saddlebags

*It is said* that when the Spaniards first arrived in Central America, the local people were frightened by the Europeans' fierce horses. The Spaniards took advantage of the situation by telling the locals that the horses would be fine as long as they were fed. They also said that the horses ate none other than gold and would not eat while being observed.

bursting with gold nuggets, they told of an incredible cache of wealth just waiting to be gathered up. Before riding off for another load, they mentioned a landmark . . . a pinnacle of rock. The soldiers failed to return from this second trip to the mine, and their bodies were eventually discovered by a search party.

In 1931, Adolph Ruth became the last known victim of the mine's curse. Armed with what he claimed was an original Peralta map, he set out for the mountains. Since the Indians were long gone from the land, Ruth felt that he had little to fear. His headless body was recovered a short time later.

Perhaps the treasure of the Lost Dutchman's Mine still waits in the sun-baked Arizona desert. But if that is so, perhaps something else also waits for those unlucky enough to find the mine.

# Another Story of GREED

There are legends of ghost ships that ply the seas, but what about a *ship that sails the desert*? There is an old story of such a ship in the California desert. The tale goes that around 1610, because of floods, a Spanish ship carrying pearls from Mexico was able to sail far northward on the land. When the floodwaters receded, the ship was trapped inland. The crew members either starved to death or were killed by Indians.

Since that time, prospectors and tourists have occasionally claimed to see a ship on the desert under full sail. The creak of the mast and rigging is reportedly heard, as well as the songs of the sailors. Is there really a phantom ship casting about in the desert searching for a way to the sea? Does her carcass rest under the sand, along with a fabulous cask of pearls? Or did a few gullible people just spend too much time in the sun?

**Curious Rites and Customs**

# SUPERSTITION

Do you have a lucky number? Are you particularly careful on Friday the 13th? If so, you are at least a *little* superstitious, and you are in the company of many millions of people all around the world. Some other superstitions are not opening an umbrella indoors because it brings bad luck, or carrying a four-leaf clover to ensure good luck. Such beliefs are based more on tradition, habit, or fear than on fact or logic.

Some of humankind's oddest rituals and customs are cloaked in superstition. Most are harmless, but they give people the feeling of being in control over things they would otherwise feel powerless about—such as luck, love, and the future. These beliefs may influence how a person views a wide range of actions, objects, and living creatures.

The animal that has been the object of many superstitions is the cat. The black cat is said to be the favorite of witches. In fact, a witch can supposedly turn into a cat, but only nine times. It is considered bad luck to have a black cat cross your path, but if it enters your house, you must be kind to it and stroke it to prevent it from running away with the household luck. On the other hand, cats are considered to bring good luck in theaters or on ships. Kicking a cat in a theater or throwing it overboard from a ship is said to bring immediate misfortune. This sounds suspiciously like a rumor started by the animals themselves!

Numbers, too, are important to a believer—particularly the number 13. Some think it's lucky, but most do not. The next time you are in an elevator in a tall building, check to see whether there is a thirteenth floor. Many buildings don't acknowledge the number, with floors going from 12 directly to 14. One source of this fear is that at the Last Supper, Jesus Christ and his apostles numbered 13. Indeed, the crucifixion took place on a Friday, which may be one reason why Friday the 13th is the most feared of days. The Egyptians used the number 7 to represent important spiritual things, and this number is generally thought to be lucky unless you are Romanian. Being born as the seventh child in a Romanian family customarily meant that you would eventually become a vampire. The number 3 is also linked to good fortune, unless you are lighting three cigarettes on one match.

Many superstitions have become traditions and habits. The original purpose of clinking glasses before drinking a toast was to make noise and scare away evil spirits so they couldn't enter the mouth

*Q*ueen Victoria of England didn't like a lot of garlic in her food. Instead, her chef chewed a clove of garlic, then breathed on the queen's food before it was served to her.

RUBBING BEAR FAT ON YOUR HEAD WAS ONCE CONSIDERED A CURE FOR BALD- NESS.

with the drink. Blocking out evil spirits was also one of the reasons that people began to cover their mouths when they yawned.

An open umbrella inside a house may be cumbersome, but that isn't why it's supposedly unlucky. That can be traced back to its association with the sun god of Egypt. The umbrella (or parasol) was developed to shield royalty from the rays of the sun, and it was considered sacrilegious to open one in the shade.

Spilling salt was considered an unfortunate omen because salt was, in the time of the Roman Empire, extremely valuable. The wasting of such a commodity could only mean that more bad luck would follow. To undo the bad luck, it was important to throw a pinch of the spilled salt over the left shoulder. That's where evil spirits were thought to gather. In fact, the Latin word for left, *sinistre,* is the basis for the English word *sinister,* which means evil.

One of the most common superstitions is that of owning a good luck charm. This might include a horseshoe, a special coin, or perhaps a rabbit's foot. To believers, certain traits made the rabbit special, such as its ability to burrow into the earth and perhaps confer with the spirits of the under-world. So, is carrying a rabbit's foot lucky? Probably not. After all, it didn't do much good for the rabbit!

# FIERY FOOTWORK

On the island of Beqa in Fiji, a most curious rite is performed by a priest known as an *mbete* (mm-BET-ay). After prayer and intense mental preparation to bring the faithful to an almost trancelike state, the priest leads them on a barefoot stroll over a scorching pit of fiery stones.

The pit is generally about 4 feet deep and 20 feet long. It is first filled with wood and covered with smooth stones, and the wood is then set aflame. The fire is allowed to burn until the red-hot stones rest on a bed of coals. To be certain that it is hot enough, the priest throws dried leaves into the pit. If they burst into flame, the preparations are complete. The fires are usually so hot that spectators must stay 20 or 30 feet from the edge of the area, or else continuously douse themselves with water. Without hesitation, the priest and his devoted followers step onto the glowing stones and slowly walk the full length of the pit. The fire walkers are not prepared physically with any special oils or protective chemicals, but they are never burned or blistered. In fact, the skin of their feet rarely even becomes very warm. And

**THE NUMBER 13** *shows up many times in American history and on U.S. currency. There were* **13** *original colonies, and the flag has* **13** *stripes. If you look at the Great Seal on the back of an American dollar, you will find the bricks of a pyramid, stars, and arrows all numbering* **13**. *The eagle there is gripping an olive branch with* **13** *leaves and olives.*

there is no damage to their hair or clothing. Scientists are baffled and have yet to come up with a satisfactory explanation for the remarkable feat.

The origin of the practice is cloaked in myth. The ability was said to be a gift from a powerful god to a prince of the tiny island. The young man supposedly spared the life of a captured saltwater eel that turned out to be the deity in disguise. To reward him for his kindness, the god offered him immunity to fire. After preparing a ritual blaze, he told the prince to lie down among the coals. The lad was uncertain and chose to simply walk across the sizzling pit. Since

then, other islanders have readily followed in his "burning" footsteps.

Although the regional origin of the custom is now lost, fire walking is also practiced in Sri Lanka and India. European observers in the early 1900s verified that the participants walked barefoot with no preparation across stones or coals heated to temperatures of more than 900 degrees Fahrenheit.

This illustration of faith is not unique to Eastern or island cultures. A similar ability is shown by devotees of the Free Pentecostal Holiness Church of the United States. During meetings, members hold lamps of flame next to their skin or handle red-hot coals, with no ill effects. Other aspects of the service include drinking poison. Certain faithful members may allow themselves to be bitten by rattlesnakes. Church members have permitted scientists to observe such rites and, as with their fearless fire-walking counterparts, it seems to be faith alone that protects the individuals.

*Hundreds* of years ago in Arabia, those who bathed regularly were excused from paying taxes.

*The palace* of Russia's Catherine the Great had dozens and dozens of rooms, but only one bathroom.

# THE NOBLE EMPEROR
☆ ☆ ☆ ☆ *of the* ☆ ☆ ☆ ☆
# UNITED STATES

Throughout history, custom has dictated that those of noble birth were to be honored and obeyed. There are tales from every land of the excesses and eccentricities of some members of royalty. Louis XIV of France owned a selection of 1,000 wigs and employed 40 wig makers. England's Queen Elizabeth I had more than 3,000 elaborate gowns in her wardrobe. A seventeenth-century Indian ruler named Jahangir counted 12,000 elephants among his great wealth.

*In medieval England,* you could supposedly cure open sores on your body by first licking a lizard and then licking the sores.

Wealth was not the only tool lavishly employed by certain nobles to please themselves or to impress or control their subjects. Power, too, was often misused. Catherine the Great ruled Russia for 32 years after the assassination of her husband in 1762. Although she was an extraordinary leader, she was not known for her tolerance. Anyone who offended her in some minor way was forced to crouch in an outer chamber of the palace, cluck like a hen, and eat his or her food from the floor.

In 1471, a **SWISS CHICKEN** was burned at the stake for laying an unnaturally colorful egg.

In 1740, another Russian empress, Anna Ivanova, had a small palace carved entirely of ice. Even the bed was made of the frigid material. There, she forced a young prince who had angered her to live with an ugly bride of her choosing. (The tale ends well: the palace melted, and the bride and groom turned out to like each other.)

There was one self-proclaimed emperor, however, who never punished anyone. Over his 20-year "reign," Norton I, the emperor of the United States, had only one uniform at a time, and lived in a simple boarding house.

Born in England in 1819, Joshua Norton arrived in San Francisco, California, 30 years later to seek his fortune. He did well for a while, but within 10 years he was penniless. It was then that he declared himself emperor of the United States. His innocent charm and sincerity caught the fancy of the editor of a San Francisco newspaper. He agreed to print on the front page a proclamation of Norton's royal ascendency to the throne.

The idea seemed to amuse many other San Franciscans as well. The citizens were particularly pleased with the emperor's second proclamation, in which he abolished Congress because the politicians were corrupt and couldn't seem to get the job done anyway. (Shortly afterward, Norton I also made himself "Protector of Mexico." In his opinion, the government of that country wasn't handling things properly, either!)

Every day, wearing a rather shabby blue and gold army uniform and a feathered hat, Emperor Norton I would stroll through the streets of his capital city to

*In* 1360, newly crowned King Pedro of Portugal made his court pay homage to his declared queen, Inez, by kissing her hand. Unfortunately for those involved, Inez had been beheaded five years earlier. It had been on the orders of his father, the former king, because he had feared that Inez might be part of a plot against him. When Pedro took the throne, he honored his lost love by temporarily seating her beside him.

be certain that things were running smoothly. He checked that streetcars were on time and that drains were clear of rubbish. His entire entourage consisted of two scruffy, good-natured dogs. His "subjects" adored him. They bowed as he passed, and rose from their chairs if he entered a room. In fact, although he was probably unaware of it, San Franciscans contributed regularly to pay for his clothes, meals, lodging, and travel. If Norton became displeased with something, he would have it "abolished." If that something happened to be a company or government office, he would reinstate it if someone asked nicely.

For two decades, the people of San Francisco cared for and honored their gentle emperor. After his death on January 8, 1880, it took two days for 10,000 of Norton's loyal subjects to file past his coffin to pay their last respects.

# Weirder than Weird People

Perhaps some of the strangest customs involve ***courtship and marriage.*** On certain Indonesian islands, women show their affection for a man by walking up and biting him. In the Solomon Islands, a woman who was about to become the chosen bride of an official of the community was placed in a cage. There, she was guarded by her father until the day of the wedding . . . which in some cases would not take place for years.

According to superstition, ***to gain love***, you must:

*Bury a badger's foot under the bed of your love object.*

*Brush your love object's lips with the hair of a hyena.*

*Slap a mole (the animal) on its right foot.*

*Sprinkle the love object with a powder of dried hummingbird.*

*Hide the dried tongue of a turtledove in the love object's house.*

---

During the Middle Ages in Europe, thousands of people died from the ***Black Plague.*** This disease was transmitted by the bites of fleas that were carried by rats. Ironically, many superstitious people blamed cats for the disease and killed thousands of them. This only made matters worse by eliminating the natural enemy of the flea-infested rats.

---

In tales of the **old west** it is said that American Indians customarily took the scalps of their enemies. True . . . but they didn't originate the practice. It began in Europe and was known in England as early as the eleventh century. At one time, European settlers in America were paid a bounty for Indian scalps to discourage resistance. The Indians were originally the victims of scalping, not the inventors.

An old British superstition claimed that *carrying a caterpillar* prevented fever.

# THE GREAT EASTERN

The dream of Isambard Brunel was to construct the world's largest oceangoing vessel. Once it was completed, however, it proved to be a floating nightmare.

Built in London in 1857, Brunel's *Great Eastern* was an incredible achievement. From end to end, the ship was longer than two football fields, and at its widest point, it spanned 118 feet. This behemoth had an innovative double hull, divided into 10 sections, that was designed to protect the ship from sinking. The *Great Eastern* was capable of carrying 4,000 passengers with a crew of 400. It was no wonder that news of the launch attracted a crowd to the shipyard. Most ships were launched into the Thames River stern-first. Because the *Great Eastern* was too large to permit this, she was built over two huge wooden cradles that were to move her into the water broadside. During the launching ceremony, Brunel was troubled. The master shipwright had not joined the ceremony, and a strange hammering noise could be heard somewhere amidships. The ceremony went on, however, and the crowd cheered as the craft began to slide toward the water—but the cradles quickly jammed and the ship refused to budge. When crews rushed to free the ship, a workman was struck by a spinning piece of equipment and flung to his death. The launch was abandoned. Over the next few months the ship very gradually slid toward the water, and by mid-March, the *Great Eastern* was afloat at last.

The ship's reputation for ill luck continued, however. In the fall of 1859, the ship's captain complained that a hammering noise in the hull kept him awake at night. And before the journey was over, an explosion had killed five crew members and demolished the saloon.

Brunel had died before the ship took to the open sea. The new owners put the *Great Eastern* on the transatlantic route from Great Britain to New York. The first three crossings were uneventful. Had the curse run its course? On the second day of the fourth voyage, several of the crew reported the sound of hammering from deep within the ship. The weather turned bad toward evening, and in the gathering gloom the stormy sea pounded the ship broadside with mile-long waves. With a groan, the first monstrous paddle wheel tore loose. Then the second paddle wheel toppled and sank into the blackened ocean. After three long days, the engineers managed to get the propeller turning. The ship returned to port, never again to sail as a passenger ship.

After a brief stint lowering armored

telegraph cable to the sea bottom (with one disastrous attempt and one successful one) the *Great Eastern* was put up for sale to the highest bidder. For several years there were no takers. Finally, a wrecker purchased the useless hulk. Tugboat crews attached lines and began the job of towing the ship to the yard. A single watchman stayed aboard to oversee the operation. Upon hearing strange hammer blows from the hull, however, the watchman begged to be taken off. When, in 1888, the double hull was ripped open, startled workmen reportedly were greeted by a macabre sight. At the ship's heart was the skeleton of the master shipwright with his bag of tools. At long last he was free of his accidental tomb.

# The Ship That WOULDN'T SINK

As early as the 1600's explorers searched for a link between the Atlantic and Pacific oceans that wouldn't take them on the more than 10,000-mile-long southern route around the tip of South America.

In 1845, two ships under the command of Sir John Franklin of Britain were anchored off the coast of Canada, ready to begin what everyone hoped would be just such a journey of discovery. Shortly after the ships set sail, word reached England that all was going well with the voyage. That cheery message was the last one received from the unfortunate expedition.

The first rescue missions, undertaken by the British, were unsuccessful. Two American ships—the *Advance* and the *Rescue*—joined the search in 1850, but they also met with no luck. Ten years later, the *Rescue* set out again to search for answers. This time she was alone, for the *Advance* lay at the bottom of the sea. According to some sailors, this fate had befallen the *Advance* because of her association with the *Rescue*. The *Rescue* had gained a sinister reputation because several of the small ship's crew had met strange and untimely deaths while aboard her. But that didn't stop American journalist Charles Hall from using her as a storeship on a trek to find some trace of the Franklin expedition.

In 1860, Hall sailed on the *George Henry* not as a journalist but as the ship's captain. The *Rescue* was close behind. The two ships traveled north to Canada and anchored in Frobisher Bay, off Baffin Island. A short time later the sky darkened and the sea turned a lead-gray color. Nervous about the approaching storm, Captain Hall decided to transfer the men of the *Rescue* to the *George Henry*. No sooner were all hands safely aboard when a fierce gale struck with full force. Deserted by her crew, the small *Rescue* battled the churning sea and howling winds for hours. At last she was thrown onto the rocks and battered mercilessly. When the storm passed, there was no sign of the unlucky ship, and the *George Henry* sailed on alone.

The next summer, after months of useless searching, the *George Henry* once more passed through Frobisher Bay, then headed into the Hudson Strait. Ahead of them, they spotted another ship following the same course. They were pleased to have the company . . . until they drew close enough to realize the chilling truth. It was the *Rescue*. She had no sails, but she seemed to be steering a definite course, even though there was clearly no one aboard!

To add to their terror, the sailors

*Saint Elmo's fire* is a form of static electricity that crackles and seems to cling to the masts of ships. As the electricity discharges, it looks like spooky fingers of light at the tip of the mast. Ancient sailors thought the light represented the celestial twins Castor and Pollux, the protectors of seamen. If only one light (one twin) was seen in the mast, it meant disaster. Both twins meant calm seas and fair winds.

discovered that what had only a short time before been a clear sea was now a maze of floating ice pieces. The frigid chunks tapped dangerously against the *George Henry*'s wooden hull. Then fate took an even more bizarre turn. A crewman cried out in horror and pointed to the *Rescue:* she had changed course and was heading directly for them. Trapped by the ice, the *George Henry* was helpless. But just at the last moment, as if changing her mind, the *Rescue* veered away and slid silently past them into the night.

Dawn brought better seas, and the *George Henry* inched homeward. At a distance, the *Rescue* trailed behind for several days. Then, as suddenly as she had appeared, the *Rescue* turned away and sailed into oblivion, leaving only unanswered questions in her wake. Could an abandoned vessel have managed so well on the open seas? Had the *Rescue* perhaps been seeking some measure of revenge against the crew that had abandoned her? Or had the ship been steered by an unseen hand, perhaps a phantom sailor from Franklin's lost crew?

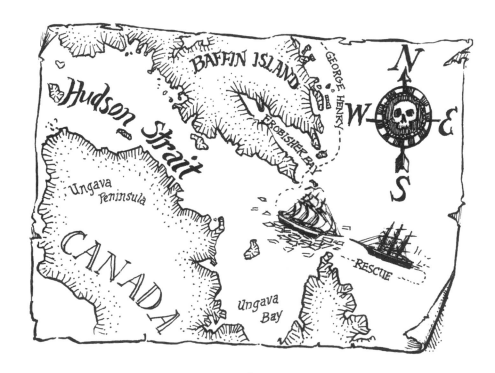

# A Voyage to Forever

Perhaps the most spine-chilling tale of the sea is that of a wretched sea captain and his phantom ship . . . the *Flying Dutchman*. According to legend, this doomed ship still sails, and sailors believe that sighting the vessel foretells disaster.

Cornelius Vanderdecken is said to have been a seventeenth-century Dutch sea captain known for taking chances and tempting fate. Unlike most sailors who had great respect for the power of wind and sea, Vanderdecken took every storm as a challenge. Risking the lives of passengers and crew, he would run full sail into gale-force winds. But one day his luck did not hold.

On a journey homeward around Africa's treacherous Cape of Good Hope, the winds were against him. Try as he might, Vanderdecken couldn't make any progress, and a storm was gathering. Only two possible courses of action existed: to turn the ship and take a course much farther out to sea, or to attempt to take a shorter—but more perilous—route close to the rocky shore. Vanderdecken ordered his crew to head toward shore. Terrified, they begged him to reconsider, but he refused. In a rage, he shoved one uncooperative sailor overboard. The others quickly obeyed.

♥

*In 1956, a lonely Swedish sailor put a message in a bottle and tossed it into the sea. It was a request for a letter from any pretty girl who might find the bottle. The Italian fisherman who actually discovered it was far from what the sailor had in mind, but the fisherman took the message to his lovely daughter. She was amused and wrote a letter to the lonesome Swede. He responded and eventually visited her—and they were married in 1958.*

♥

As the ship moved closer and closer to the dangerous rocks, the crewmen began to pray for deliverance from what was sure to be a horrible fate. Vanderdecken, too, dropped to his knees, but it was to curse God and the devil in frustration. Screaming and shaking his fist at the heavens, he vowed that he would succeed if it took until Judgment Day. Then, suddenly, a brilliant shaft of light broke through the inky clouds.

The legend goes that a shimmering shape settled on the deck and spoke angrily. Vanderdecken would, indeed, sail until Judgment Day. From that day forward, the ship would travel without rest. The spirit then disappeared, and suddenly Vanderdecken's ship moved easily against the storm. It is said that the winds have filled its sails ever since and that never again will the captain or crew enjoy the comfort of any port.

# More from the Realm of Neptune

~~~~~~~~~~~~~~~~~~~~~~~~~~~~

⚓ During World War I, a **British submarine** cruising just below the surface made an unusual sighting. The sub's second officer was gazing into the periscope, searching for any sign of danger, when he suddenly saw a lone man bobbing in the waves and signaling to him. He recognized the sailor as an officer on a ship that had been presumed lost at sea several weeks earlier. Without questioning how the man could have survived, the captain ordered the submarine to surface. The crew members scrambled on deck and frantically scanned the area, but at first saw nothing. Then, with a cry, a sailor pointed to something floating in the water. Two deadly mines were directly in their intended path—mines that the submarine would have hit if the vessel had not been beckoned to the surface.

⚓ In 1961, a **reward** was offered by the tourist board of the Isle of Man to anyone who could capture a live mermaid.

REWARD

FOR CAPTURE OF LIVE MERMAID

# 40 *minutes*
# IN A THUNDERCLOUD

It was July 26, 1959. Lt. Colonel William Rankin was planning to make a routine flight in his F8-U Crusader fighter jet from Massachusetts to North Carolina. Unfortunately, he was about to experience a thunderstorm in a way that no one else ever had. He was flying at about 47,000 feet when he detected a curious noise from the engine. Warning lights flashed as the plane lost power. Although he was directly over an ominous black thunderhead, Rankin knew he had to eject from the stricken jet.

With no protective clothing other than a light flight suit, boots, gloves, and a helmet, the pilot immediately felt the excruciating effects of the air temperature of 70 degrees below zero. The change in air pressure caused his body to undergo a painful decompression that was lessened only when, within seconds, he entered the denser atmosphere at the upper levels of the thunderhead.

A moment later, Rankin's chute opened, and he felt himself relax. The ordeal would soon be over, he thought. But suddenly, he was jerked hundreds of feet back up into the air, as if he were nothing more than a rag doll, only to plummet once more into a churning maelstrom of dark clouds. Once the storm had him in its grasp, it tossed him up and down and from side to side. The terrified pilot tried to hold his breath because, he said, "All this time it had been raining so torrentially that I thought I would drown in midair."

Mercifully, Rankin finally dropped below the seething storm and glimpsed solid ground. Then, as a final insult, the wind sent him crashing into the trunk of a tree. Remarkably, though, he had made it to the ground in one piece. Rankin suffered a myriad of cuts, bruises, strains, and sprains. He had difficulty gaining his balance, and even experienced amnesia for a short time, but he considers himself very lucky. He had spent a total of 40 minutes, alone and unprotected, deep within the heart of a thunderstorm.

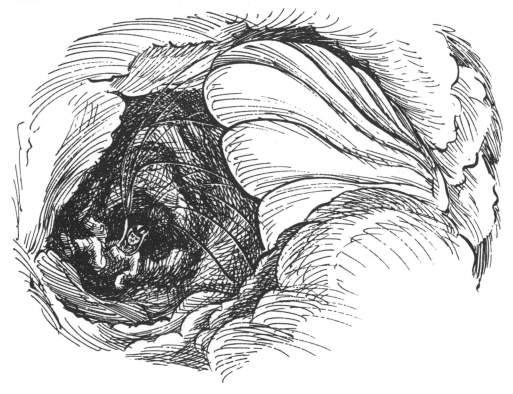

# IN HARM'S WAY

IN HARM'S WAY

*A Kenyan man* by the name of Musyoka Mututa had *four funerals* over his lifetime. The first was when he was 3, the second when he was 19, and the third took place years later in May 1985 when Mututa was an adult. In each case he was pronounced dead, but as he was *being lowered* to the ground he *revived.* The final funeral was in September 1985. To be certain it was necessary, the family kept the body *above ground* for two days.

The power of nature can be ruinous and often deadly. Every year, hundreds of people lose their lives in earthquakes, floods, and violent storms such as tornadoes.

Although it is usually short-lived and difficult to predict, the tornado is the most powerful of Earth's storms. Its whirling winds may reach speeds of 300 miles or more per hour. Tornadoes have been known to lift cars, shatter buildings, shred trees into splinters, and twist metal bars or project them through solid stone. It may seem as though a human being has little chance against such might, but two men have actually looked up into the very heart of such a storm, and survived.

The first was farmer Will Keller of Greensburg, Kansas. On a warm day early in the summer of 1928, Keller was working in his fields. Glancing up from his labor, he spotted a coal-black twister roaring toward him across the open plain. He dashed to his house and ordered his family into the storm cellar. When everyone was safe, Keller, too, headed for the shelter. As he was about to close and secure the storm door behind him, he took a last look at the tornado and noted that the funnel had left the ground. Tornadoes sometimes skip over depressions or irregular areas, then slam back into the ground with full force. Keller bravely took the risk and waited to view something that no one on record had ever seen. As the storm passed overhead, he looked directly up into the funnel. A wall of black clouds whirled around the open heart of the tornado. The interior was lit up eerily as lightning flashed and crackled within. Tiny, hissing funnels were spawned from the main body, and then spun off on their own. Keller also noticed a strong, gassy odor.

Roy Hall of McKinney, Texas, found himself in a similar situation in 1943. Trying to find shelter from an oncoming tornado, Hall had dropped to the ground. Clutching his young child, he covered the youngster protectively with his body and prepared for the worst. In this case, too, the twister left the ground, and the raging storm passed directly above. In a few seconds that must have felt like an eternity, Hall stared into the inside of the funnel, which he said looked like "the interior of a glazed pipe." It appeared slick, and the swirling wall of inky-black clouds was no more than 10 feet thick. The inside was lit by lightning. High up and at the center, the tornado was spinning around a glowing cloud.

▲

*In 1985, a motorcycle accident left Richard Topps of Derbyshire, England, impaled on a four-foot-long wooden fence post. Although the post pierced his body from chest to hip, it missed all vital organs. After lengthy surgery to remove the post, Topps was fine.*

▼

Not all survivors of a tornado volunteer for the encounter. In 1931, a powerful twister hoisted a more than 80-ton train into the air like a toy. It lifted the train 80 feet, then dashed it into a ditch, killing many of the more than 100 passengers. In 1955, the occupants of a car in Illinois were luckier. With the two terror-stricken travelers inside, a tornado lifted the vehicle 100 feet into the air and set it safely back to earth. Perhaps the oddest example of the unpredictability of a tornado, however, is the behavior of one that struck in Ancona, Italy, in 1981. The victim was a baby asleep in his carriage. The twister lifted the carriage 50 feet up and carried it for 300 feet, then set it down so gently that the child didn't even wake up from his nap!

Hundreds of thousands of people have come to the very brink of death and, with the aid of modern medicine, have survived. Some have reportedly even crossed that precipice for an extremely short time . . . and returned. Hundreds of people who have been pronounced dead and have then been revived claim to have had what is called a near-death experience, or NDE. This seems to take many different forms, but a few common details are mentioned over and over.

First, the patient describes the sensation of floating above his or her own body and watching the action below. Often, the scene is at the site of an accident or in a hospital room. Some claim that they tried to speak to or touch doctors or loved ones, but to no avail. One young boy, for example, had suffered critical injuries when he was struck by a car while riding his bicycle. He later explained that he had watched from above as a crowd gathered and had witnessed many people trying to help him. He even saw the ambulance and followed it for a short distance.

NDEs have also been reported to include traveling through a dark tunnel toward a bright light; seeing beautiful,

> ➤ *A condemned criminal was actually executed but was then revived. In 1650, in England, Ann Greene was hanged for murder. Her body remained suspended for about 30 minutes. When she was taken down, she revived. Authorities took it as a reprieve and released her.* ➤

**IN 1978,**
*American Henry Sims was awakened from a sound sleep by the frantic cries of his young nephew. Sims immediately realized that his home was on fire. He managed to wake other family members, and everyone escaped safely. Sim's nephew, however, had died in a fire 46 years earlier.*

glowing beings who give off a sense of being loving and helpful; viewing a beautiful, sunny meadow; meeting long-dead relatives and friends; and, finally, being told that it is not the right time and that they must return to life.

Needless to say, there is a great deal of controversy about the subject of NDEs. Although most researchers feel that patients who claim to have had such experiences are being truthful, some believe that they are simply hallucinating. Others, however, offer evidence in support of NDEs, and the following story provides an example of this.

A woman identified only as Mary related her own experience after suffering a heart attack and being rushed to the hospital. Doctors managed to stabilize her condition, and it seemed as though she would fully recover. Within a few hours, however, she suffered a second attack. Doctors and nurses rushed to her side and although they worked feverishly to save her, they appeared to be losing the battle. Finally, however, Mary's heartbeat returned to normal, and a wave of relief washed through the room as it became clear that she had survived once again.

Later, when a hospital worker came by to chat with the recovering patient, Mary told her an unusual story. She claimed that as the medical team was working to save her, she felt herself drifting free of her body. She floated slowly toward the ceiling, watching the scene with detached curiosity. Then she continued to move, unimpaired by doors or walls. She found herself outside the building. Passing a third-floor ledge, she had noticed a sneaker balanced there that was noticeably worn where the small toe would have been. As she noted that the laces were tucked under the shoe, she felt herself being drawn back to her hospital room, faster and faster. When she awoke, Mary was once again in her bed looking up at her doctor.

The hospital worker felt that this was the tale of a woman who had been under incredible stress. She knew that Mary had not been in any condition to roam around the hospital and could not have been up to the third floor,

E leven-year-old Nick Christides had planned to just catch a few waves and call it a day. Nevertheless, while surfing off the shores of Australia's Cocos Island in the Indian Ocean, he was caught by powerful currents and dragged out to sea. He was recovered four hours later, frightened, but in fine health because of a friend. Throughout most of the terrifying experience, a lone dolphin had not only protected the boy from dangerous sharks but had buoyed him up when he was in danger of sinking.

particularly from the outside. Nevertheless, when she left the room, the hospital worker decided to check the third-floor ledge. After looking out from several vantage points, she was convinced that her own feeling was correct. But just to be sure, she tried one more room. There, as she leaned against the glass of the window, she was amazed to see a sneaker on the ledge. The lace was under the heel. The hospital worker couldn't see the side that had been described by Mary, so she opened the window and brought the sneaker inside. Then she ran her fingers over the worn area located in the spot over the little toe. She knew that was a detail that could only have been noticed by someone viewing the shoe from the *outside* of the building.

# ..........HOW BIZARRE!..........

☞ In 1885, a British man by the name of **John Lee** was convicted of murder and sentenced to hang. He was led to the scaffold, but he had nothing to say when asked if he had any last words. The rope was placed around his neck, and he stood on the trapdoor that would soon drop out from beneath him. Or maybe not. The door wouldn't budge.

Authorities tried three separate times. Between each attempt they tested the door, which worked perfectly until Lee stood on it. Before the last attempt, they even shaved the edges to prevent it from sticking, but the trapdoor simply wouldn't work with the condemned man in place. Lee's sentence was changed to life in prison. He was later released and moved to the United States.

☞ James Bartley, a sailor on a whaling ship in 1891, was part of a longboat crew trying to subdue a huge, harpooned sperm whale. In a valiant effort to save itself, the whale hurtled upward and smashed the small boat. The whale died, and all of the sailors were pulled from the sea . . . all, that is except Bartley. On the whaling ship, the body of the whale was cut open for processing. Bartley's shipmates were astounded to find him in the animal's stomach, unconscious but alive.

Now Exiting Weirdsville

We hope you enjoyed your visit!

Watch the dark rooms you enter and the sharp corners you turn, for you never know when you may end up back in Weirdsville.

We'll be waiting for you . . . .